# PEEKS at the PAST

## in Sheffield and the surrounding area

By Ann Beedham

The Anglican Church in Sheffield General Cemetery

Copyright Pickard Publishing, 10-11 Riverside Park, Sheaf Gardens, Sheffield S2 4BB
telephone 0114 2757222 or 2757444 facsimile 0114 2758866 email info@picomm.co.uk
Illustrations, graphics and photographs by Ann Beedham unless otherwise stated

# Contents

When wandering around places, I invariably trip up or fall down a kerb or pothole. This is because I am usually too busy looking up at buildings or aspects of architecture or artwork that take my eye. I like seeing the details - a little gargoyle, an interesting doorway, a stone face with wistful expression.

This book is a peek at the past which is lost in the modern bustle we live in today - the old statue passed without a second glance by shoppers, or the Cutlers' elephant looking down at supertram. It is a look at some of these features and a little of the history connected with them; also some of the people that helped create that history.

It is not meant to be an in depth discussion of a person or place, but to remind people of the wealth of history, beauty and artwork that is around them. It will perhaps encourage readers to notice afresh the unsung and forgotten corners they pass each day.

Whilst talking to various people I have been amazed at their knowledge and enthusiasm and am grateful for the help they gave. Many readers will know far more about the history of our area than I - so apologies in advance if you find any mistakes or anything to disagree with. I have tried to check with various sources any facts mentioned and in doing so had correspondence with many interesting people. I have also visited new places and discovered some interesting things, or looked at the known with new eyes. I hope you do too.

**Ann Beedham**

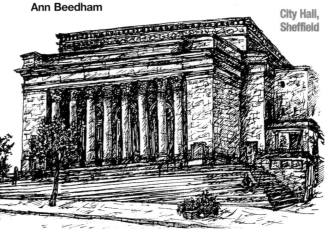

City Hall, Sheffield

**This book is dedicated to my father, John (Jack) Beedham**

# The Town Hall Sheffield

**A proud focus of Sheffield City Centre is the splendid edifice of the Town Hall, with the clock tower gazing down on the busy Fargate shopping precinct...**

The Town Hall is a well known feature, with the green oasis of the Peace Gardens and the new Winter Gardens taking shape around it. The present Town Hall was built to replace the one on the corner of Castle Street and Waingate, near the markets.

The Town Hall being built 1896

## First steps

In 1886, the council acquired land to build a new town hall and the council launched a competition for architects to design the building. Mr E.W. Mountford's design was chosen from 178 submissions. The person chosen to carry out and supervise the carving was Mr F.W. Pomeroy. The foundation stone was laid on October 9, 1891, by the mayor of the time, William Johnson Clegg.

A view of the town hall showing some of the exterior carvings (an eagle and an owl).

## The opening

The building was officially opened on 21st May, 1897, by Queen Victoria, with pomp and crowds.

Only four years later, in 1901, it was decided the building was too small and plans for an extension were begun, with Mountford to design it again. A lack of finance and the outbreak of World War 1 curtailed any plans for this, however, and it wasn't until 1923 that the extension was finally built. The newer part is to the rear of the building and blends in so well it is difficult to distinguish it from the original.

Queen Victoria at the Opening Ceremony. The round tokens shown above were given out as souvenirs

## The tower

The grand clock tower reaches 64 metres high. At the top stands a figure of Vulcan, the mythical god of fire. This character is a fitting symbol for the city that gave birth to the steel industry. The clock faces are 2.5 metres in diameter.

## Vulcan

The bronze statue of Vulcan atop the Town Hall clock tower was made by a sculptor named Mario Raggi in 1897. He holds a hammer and arrows and stands upon an anvil. It is said to be modelled from a Lifeguardsman.

Vulcan has given his name to many things, volcanoes and planes, as well as the home planet of Mr Spock in science fiction series Star Trek.

He used to feature in the old Star newspaper masthead, inside a six pointed star. This was used as a logo until 1959. A column in the newspaper was called 'Vulcan speaks', then just 'Vulcan', and stayed as a feature until 1988.

Right: A drawing from The Star newspaper, of Vulcan defiant after the Blitz, Monday Dec.16, 1940. Below: The old Star masthead, used until 1959

Vulcan on the clock tower

DEFIANT!

The ★ Star
21.991   THURSDAY, JUNE 6, 1957   A KEMSLEY NEWSPAPER.   2|4.

1

Peeks at the Past

## The frieze

Above the main entrance is engraved the city coat of arms. Above that is a statue of Queen Victoria and the Royal coat of arms. Along the exterior of the building is a frieze containing figures representing the industries of Sheffield. On the right hand side is a woman carrying a cornucopia, or horn of plenty, representing the fruits of labour.

Next are those labours; smiths, grinders, smelters and miners. On the left is a woman carrying a blazing torch, representing the light of knowledge. Next to her are sculptors, painters, metalworkers, buffers and finishers. Figures representing electricity and steam decorate the main entrance. On the Surrey Street entrance are figures representing war and peace.

## The gates

The impressive, wrought iron gates were also designed by Mountford. When Queen Victoria opened the Town Hall, she stayed in her carriage as she was infirm. Electricity was still a new and unknown quantity to many, but was used in the ceremony. The Queen was handed a special box in which she turned a key and used this amazing new power to 'open the gates'. In fact the key in this special box did not move the gates at all - it switched on a light bulb inside the building, alerting some men to open the gates by hand as a pre-arranged signal was given!

The six statues in the main entrance are by Pomeroy and depict the virtues. The captions read:

> *"Be just and fear not - Work while it is day for the night cometh - God shall rule and guide our councils - Better it is to get wisdom than gold - Let all things be done with charity - Strength and temperance will enforce the law."*

## The main hall

The archways are the main feature, with detailed carvings, a fitting setting for the grand staircase made of Sicilian marble, with balustrades made of alabaster. A high dome lets in natural light and suspended from this is a bronze 'electrolier' light. This is in the design of a globe, with signs of the zodiac and four angels. It caused a stir at the opening as people queued to see the miracle of electricity at work. The walls are of veined Derbyshire and Devonshire marble. Over the main archway is a scene said to depict the local legend of the Dragon of Wharncliffe, not St. George and the Dragon as many think.

These old measuring guides are next to the Town Hall, on the right hand side on Cheney Row. They were moved there from St. Paul's Parade when the Peace Gardens were redeveloped

The legend is believed to refer to Wortley and Wharncliffe, when the Earls of Wharncliffe and More Hall were engaged in a power struggle for land. The coat of arms of More Hall contains a dragon.

A seahorse carving on the arch above the main entrance

The statue at the foot of the staircase is of the first Lord Mayor of Sheffield, the 15th Duke of Norfolk. He is wearing the dress of a Knight of the Garter.

## Other rooms

Near the top of the staircase is the entrance to the Ante Room of the Council Chamber. This room contains photographs of all the previous Lord Mayors. At the head of the staircase is the Grand Corridor (46 metres long), also lined with marble. Off this corridor are the Lord Mayor's Parlour and the reception rooms, which have ornate coloured plaster ceilings. A door from the centre reception room leads out on to the Town Hall balcony.

In the Council Chamber is the ceremonial chair used by the Lord Mayor. It is beneath a carved oak structure or pediment, made in 1896, which bears the Coat of Arms and is supported by four oak pillars. The carving is mainly floral, with oak, ash, ivy, rose, thistle and shamrock. In front of the chair is a bench, which has a carved centrepiece depicting two children rising from tree branches and bears the motto "work while it is day".

The grand frontage of the Town Hall

Above is an angel from the Town Hall frontage, carrying a hammer and arrows, a reminder of Sheffield's ancient arrow making heritage.

## The Civic Regalia

### The Lord Mayor's Chain

This was bought by public subscription in 1856 and cost £325. It is made of 18 carat gold and weighs 50 oz. In the centre is the city coat of arms in enamel. The chain has 27 links, simulating tied ribbons. Each is inscribed with the names of past Mayors. There are never more than 27 links on the chain, as new ones are added, some older ones are taken off and placed in a display cabinet in the Lord Mayor's Parlour.

### The Lord Mayor's Badge

This is worn when the heavy chain is impractical to wear. It was of 18 carat gold made by Mappin and Webb, presented in 1908. It has an enamel city coat of arms and is decorated with diamonds, amethysts and white Brazilian topaz.

The Lord Mayor's Chain

Photograph from the Star

### The Lady Mayoress's Chain

This was first presented by Lord Mayor George Senior in 1901 and his wife was the first to wear it. It is made of 18 carat gold and weighs 34oz. The Royal Arms form the main part, and the arms of the city are suspended from this by a chain of finely wrought white roses, representing Yorkshire. As with the Mayor's chain, it has 27 links bearing names of past Lady Mayoresses.

### The Lady Mayoress's Badge

This was first made in 1929 by Mappin and Webb at a cost of £31. However, the original was lost and the present badge was made in 1976. It is made of 18 carat gold and has the Sheffield Shield in enamel in the centre, with white roses as decoration.

### The Mace

This was presented to the city by the Duke of Norfolk to commemorate his becoming the first Lord Mayor. It is made entirely of silver and is 402 inches long. This mace is carried before the Lord Mayor on public occasions, as real maces or weapons used to be. It is designed like a crown, and has oak leaf, acorn, pomegranate and Yorkshire Rose decorations. It bears the same latin motto as the Coat of Arms as well as the inscription 'Omar Ramsden and Alwyn CE Carr made me in the Year of our Lord 1899'.

### The Eggbox

Also now a thing of the past is the huge concrete mass of the later Town Hall extension, nicknamed the 'eggbox' because of its shape. It was demolished early 2002 to make way for new developments, including a hotel and was knocked down as the arches of the new Winter Gardens were taking shape behind it.

Based on text supplied by Sheffield City Council

### The City Coat of Arms

This was granted to the Sheffield Borough Council on 16th July, 1875, and to the present City Council on 1st September 1977.

The image shows at the top a rampant lion, a symbol from the arms of the Duke of Norfolk, who was the first Lord Mayor.

On the large shield in the centre are a sheaf of arrows, which is an old symbol from the seals used in Sheffield by the *Burgesses,* who ran the city before the Council.

Also on the shield are three sheaves of wheat, on a green background representing a field. This is a play upon the name Sheffield, which means *"the open space by the River Sheaf."*

Supporting the shield are two figures.

On the left is Thor, the smith and thunder god of the Scandinavians, with his hand resting on a hammer.

On the right is Vulcan, the fire smith god of the Greek and Romans, standing in front of an anvil and holding a set of pincers. He also stands atop the Town Hall clock tower.

These are appropriate guardians for a city steeped in the life of using fire to create steel.

On the banner at the bottom are the Latin words *"Deo Adjuvante Labor Proficit",* which means 'with God's help our labour is successful."

## Around the Town Hall

### The Peace Gardens

Here once stood St Paul's Church, next to the Town Hall. It was a classical style building, opened in 1740. It was demolished in 1936. The 'Peace Gardens' opened on the site two years later.

St. Paul's church

Demolition

### The New Peace Gardens

The present new development of fountain, cascades and walkways replaced the old Peace Gardens. There are lovely leaf carvings and coloured tiles in the water channels, as well as huge water spouts representing steel flowing, and carved fishes dotted around the stone walls. The large, multi height fountain provides a stunning display.

### The Moor

This busy thoroughfare, now a main shopping destination, used to be called South Street through the 19th century as it formed the main route south. In February 1922 it was given the name it holds now, reflecting its origins as the area first called Sheffield Moor, being a route across the moor to the town centre.

In the 1970's it was pedestrianised. The aztec type office building was built across the foot of the Moor, with its iron gates that were to be a walk through but seem never to open.

On the Moor, at the junction with Rockingham Way, is a poem by poet Berlie Doherty, carved by calligrapher Celi Kilner:

*Here lies a city's heart.*
*There in her hills lie her green bones.*
*Quiet under the clutter of*
*houses and streets,*
*And there in her rivers run veins*
*That long ago powered her mills,*
*Her long limbs reach to the moors.*
*But here, here lies her throbbing heart."*

### Jubilee Monument

This obelisk (seen in front of the Town Hall just to the right of the clock tower) was erected in 1887 to celebrate Queen Victoria's Diamond Jubilee. It now stands in Endcliffe Park, near Hunters Bar. It was replaced by a statue of Victoria which now also stands in the same park.

### Sheffield Citadel

On the right as you walk down the Moor, on Cross Burgess Street, stands a red castellated building, built in 1892, for The Salvation Army.

Rev william Booth, founder of the Salvation Army, sent one of his evangelists, Capt. Mary Goddard, to Sheffield in 1878, accompanied by her husband and a Miss Dunnage, plus a man known as Gypsy Smith. They founded a place to meet, in the Temperance Hall which used to be on Townhead Street. (This later became the Playhouse Theatre). Booth visited

Sheffield a few times to see how his flock were getting on. In fact he became caught up in Sheffield Riots in 1882. when many of the Salvation Army were set upon, or had things thrown at them. Many local people at the time were against the movement and the Salvation Army officers often suffered abuse. But things improved and membership grew. Eventually the Temperance Hall was too small. The Army often rented the Albert Hall, (this used to be in Barkers Pool where Cole Brothers is now – it burned down in 1937) for bigger gatherings.

In September 1892, the foundation stone was laid for their own Citadel Hall. Around 7000-8,000 people watched, spilling down Pinstone Street and as far as the railings of St. Paul's Church. The corner site project included building shops too, and cost around £25,000 altogether. On Pinstone Street, in stonework above the shops, the letters SA can still be seen, showing where an entrance into the building used to be.

The Citadel at the time of writing is up for sale, probably to be converted to a bar or offices. The Salvation Army has moved to a new location on Psalter Lane.

# Arbor Low

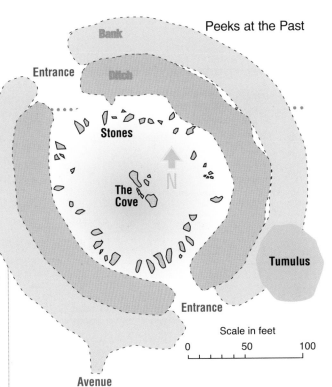

A spectacular 4000 year old prehistoric monument lies in the fields of Derbyshire, spread upon the grass like a huge, silent clockface...

Set in a field behind a farm, near Monyash, is an ancient stone circle, or henge. It is known as the Stonehenge of the North and consists of a bank 250ft in diameter, about 7ft high, with a 30ft wide, 5ft deep quarry ditch.

## The Mighty Henge

This enigmatic monument, 1,200ft above sea level, is one of the county's chief prehistoric monuments. Recumbent limestones lie surrounded by a ditch in a wild and open place.

The ditch is broken by two entrances, and encloses a circle of around 40 stones, none of which is standing. The largest stone is about 13ft long. The name Arbor Low is thought to derive from the Anglo Saxon *Eorthburh Hlaw*, which merely means earthwork hill. This ancient structure would have amazed people through the centuries. When the Romans arrived, the site was already 2,500 years old.

It is not known whether the stones were originally upright. In 1758 it is recorded that one man remembered the stones standing, but when the circle was excavated no evidence of holes that the stones would have rested in was found. It could be that no deep pits were dug to stand them in so no traces are left. If they were just set in shallow foundations, this could explain why they have all fallen, with many of the stones breaking on impact with the ground. There are some stumps of stone which could support this theory, being the lower broken part of the recumbent stones. It is an exposed site so loosely set stones could have blown over. At the centre is a U shaped cluster of stones, called the cove. This has two of the biggest stones. Near these stones a male skeleton was found.

No one knows why these henges, the most famous of which is Stonehenge, were built. Perhaps they were the enclosures for rituals or communal gatherings. Some people think they were used for astronomical calculations.

## Around Arbor Low

Close to the area of the monument are found burial mounds, or barrows. One such barrow is built into the bank near the Southern entrance of the ditch. This was excavated by local historian Thomas Bateman, in 1845. In it he found cremations, a bone pin and two food vessels within a cist (small enclosure of stones).

A shoulder-blade and an antler of a large red deer were found and, in a cist in the centre were discovered human bones, a kidney-shaped piece of flint, a pin made from the leg bone of a small deer and a spherical piece of iron pyrites. At the west end of the cist were two clay urns, shaped and decorated in very different ways plus a fragment of a third.

In 1901-2 Arbor Low was excavated again, this time by a man called H. St George Gray. He dug the bank and ditch and found flint tools, ox bones, 2 arrowheads and traces of fires.

> "The 23rd of May, 1845, is an important day in the annuals of barrow-digging in Derbyshire, as on that day was made the discovery...of the original internment in the large tumulus which forms one side of the southern entrance to the temple of Arbor Lowe."
>
> **Thomas Bateman**

## Gib Hill

A low bank and ditch, that may have been built at a later date, run towards Arbor Low from the south. Also, 350 yards to the south lies a mount known as Gib Hill. This is a large barrow, about 10ft high. This is how Bateman describes it:

*"Its height, immense size and remote antiquity are calculated to impress the reflecting mind with feelings of wonder and admiration."*

The name may come from the fact that a gibbet was once placed on the mound, but nobody knows for sure. It seems to have been built in two phases. An earlier neolithic (4000 - 2000 BC) oval barrow was enlarged by building a mound over the top of it. This mound was probably built in the early Bronze age, (2000 - 700 BC).

In this mound Bateman found a stone cist containing a cremation and a food vessel, as well as an arrow-head of flint, two and a half inches long. The cist had probably been placed on top of the earlier barrow, before the bigger mound was put on top. When the excavation was taking place, the cist, with its heavy stones, crashed down and crushed a food vessel and the remains of the human cremation which had been inside it. Bateman put this central stone cist in his home grounds in a village nearby, but it has now been re-erected and the capstone is just visible at the crest of the barrow.

To the north west of Gib Hill there are traces of a 180ft diameter ditched enclosure and bank that may be another henge monument. The site is managed by English Heritage: Northampton Office NN1 1UH

There is a request for a donation of 50p, which can be left in a tin by the farm. There is a small car park.

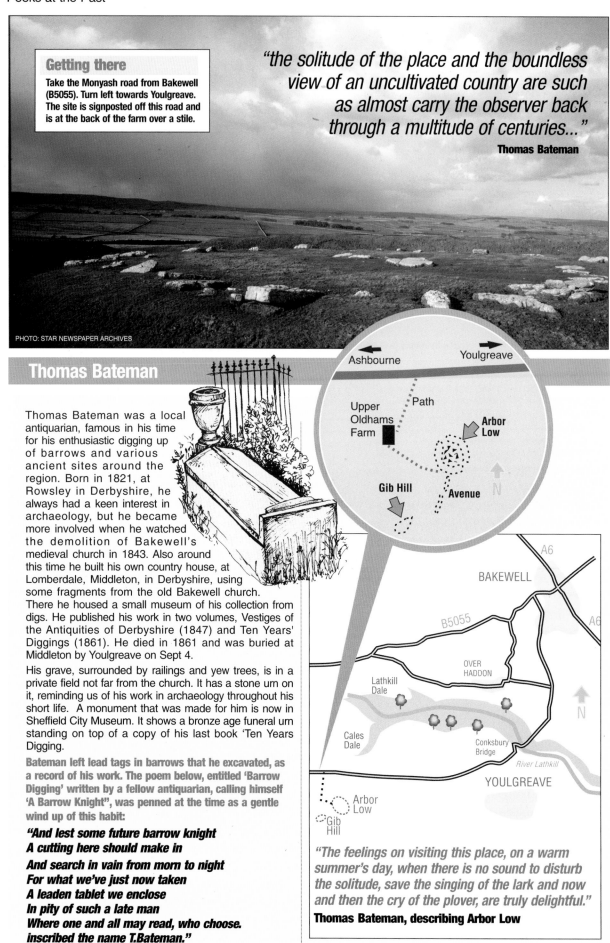

## Getting there

Take the Monyash road from Bakewell (B5055). Turn left towards Youlgreave. The site is signposted off this road and is at the back of the farm over a stile.

*"the solitude of the place and the boundless view of an uncultivated country are such as almost carry the observer back through a multitude of centuries..."*

**Thomas Bateman**

## Thomas Bateman

Thomas Bateman was a local antiquarian, famous in his time for his enthusiastic digging up of barrows and various ancient sites around the region. Born in 1821, at Rowsley in Derbyshire, he always had a keen interest in archaeology, but he became more involved when he watched the demolition of Bakewell's medieval church in 1843. Also around this time he built his own country house, at Lomberdale, Middleton, in Derbyshire, using some fragments from the old Bakewell church.

There he housed a small museum of his collection from digs. He published his work in two volumes, Vestiges of the Antiquities of Derbyshire (1847) and Ten Years' Diggings (1861). He died in 1861 and was buried at Middleton by Youlgreave on Sept 4.

His grave, surrounded by railings and yew trees, is in a private field not far from the church. It has a stone urn on it, reminding us of his work in archaeology throughout his short life. A monument that was made for him is now in Sheffield City Museum. It shows a bronze age funeral urn standing on top of a copy of his last book 'Ten Years Digging.

Bateman left lead tags in barrows that he excavated, as a record of his work. The poem below, entitled 'Barrow Digging' written by a fellow antiquarian, calling himself 'A Barrow Knight", was penned at the time as a gentle wind up of this habit:

*"And lest some future barrow knight*
*A cutting here should make in*
*And search in vain from morn to night*
*For what we've just now taken*
*A leaden tablet we enclose*
*In pity of such a late man*
*Where one and all may read, who choose.*
*inscribed the name T.Bateman."*

*"The feelings on visiting this place, on a warm summer's day, when there is no sound to disturb the solitude, save the singing of the lark and now and then the cry of the plover, are truly delightful."*
**Thomas Bateman, describing Arbor Low**

## Around Stanton Moor

### Nine Ladies and Stanton Moor

The other most famous stone circle in the Peak area is that of the Nine Ladies. It stands in a sheltered hollow near the northern end of Stanton Moor, near Stanton in Peak, off the A6. The circle in fact consists of ten stones, about 2 to 3 feet in height. 30ft in diameter, its purpose is unknown. The name Nine Ladies was given before a tenth stone in the bank was uncovered due to erosion in the last 15 years. About 130ft from the circle is the 3ft high 'King Stone' set on its own. A legend tells that the stones are ladies turned to rock for dancing on the sabbath and the King Stone was their fiddler.

Around sixty burial mounds have been found on the moor, often with cremation urns and flint tools. They were excavated many years ago by local archaeologist J C Heathcote and his son J P Heathcote.

An old print of Nine Ladies circle on Stanton Moor

**Carvings.** On some of the rocks on Stanton Moor are carvings, including a deeply cut letter Y and a coronet with the date 1826. This is to commemorate the Duke of York. These carvings were put there by the Thornhill Family of nearby Stanton Hall.

### Earl Grey Tower.

Also to be found on the moor is a 30ft high. square brick tower (left). This was built in tribute to Earl Grey, who carried the reform bill through parliament. Over the door is inscribed his name and the date 1832. Nearby are the Duke of York stone, with a coronet and the inscription Y 1826. and one inscribed G 1834.

Right: an urn found in one of the burial mounds on Stanton Moor

PHOTO: STAR ARCHIVES

### The Cork Stone

On the western side of the moor is a large stone with holes that have been added to aid climbing up to the top of it. This is known as the Cork Stone.

### Rowter Rocks

Near to Stanton Moor, at the bottom end of the village of Birchover, and behind the Druid Inn, are some amazing rocks. These gritstone features have natural rock basins, though the hand of man has added quirky 'improvements'. Some large stones as you climb the path at the back of the Druid Inn have socket marks on. These may indicate that wooden structures were built here, with these holes made for putting the poles in.

As you wander around these fascinating rocks you can see carved out chambers. Some tales say these were part of a prison for those awaiting druidical sacrifice. There is no evidence of this, however.

The Rev. Thomas Eyre, who lived close by in the 17th century, converted these rocks into a retreat.

He carved rooms, arm chairs and steps to link the different areas together.

The Cork Stone

Some of the carved stairs at Rowter Rocks, in Birchover

## Other Circles in The Peak

### Nine Stone Close, the Hermits Cave and Robin Hood's Stride

On Harthill Moor, off the road from Bakewell to Winster (B5056), and not far from The Druid Inn, is found the stone circle called Nine Stone Close. Contrary to the name, there are now only four large stones left, one being eight feet high and nine feet in circumference. One stone is in use nearby as a gatepost. There is no public access to the stones. If you wish to visit, ask at the farm opposite to seek permission.

Overlooking the stones is a natural rock outcrop called Robin Hood's Stride.

Another name for it is Mock Beggars' Hall, as the shape resembles a hall with tall chimneys. These 'chimneys' are 18ft high and 22ft apart.

Also nearby stands a rock formation called Cratcliffe Tors. A path here winds to an old hermit's cave with a crucifix carved upon the right hand wall. The carving is unusual as it has foliage carved around the cross.

The cave is hidden behind the boughs of an ancient yew.

Also in the cave is a small niche, probably to hold a lamp.

The old shelter is thought to be from the fourteenth century. perhaps used as a stop off on the ancient trackway called the Portway, which passes between the tor and Robin Hood's Stride.

Nine Stone Close, with Robin Hood's Stride in the background

Crucifix carving from the wall at hermit's cave on Cratcliffe Tors

### Barbrook Circles

Other stone circles in the area are those on Barbrook Moor, off to the right through white gates on the A621 Owler Bar to Baslow road.

The first encountered to the right of the footpath from the road is Barbrook I. It is an isolated spot, very atmospheric and hardly any signs of man can be seen from here, even though the road is so close. It consists of a ring of 12 stones, all around 2ft high, with a damaged low bank around them.

About 800ft further on from Barbrook I is Barbrook II. It consists of a rubble bank, with a ring of standing stones set along the inside of it. These are all under 2ft high, except for one which is 3ft high. The bank has an original entrance about 10ft wide to the north east. In the centre of the circle is a small cairn and a cist, both from around 1800BC, (mid Bronze Age).

There are other circles on the moor but they are harder to find. Although there is a path, the circles are in a wildlife sanctuary, so please respect this. The area is managed by Peak District National Park Authority. Contact them if you wish to visit the circles.

### Youlgreave

The village of Youlgreave lies a little way from Birchover between the Bradford and Lathkill rivers and was once a centre for lead mining, then gritstone quarrying.

The dominating feature of this pretty place is the church, All Saints. It is partly Norman, with a 14th century tower.

The font here is late Norman period. It is unusual as it has an extra holder on the side, for putting in oil. This is called a stoop. A wonderful dragon or salamander carving decorates the stone. The font is said to have come from the nearby village of Elton, which later wanted it back but had to settle for a copy.

Another feature of the church is

The old font with its unusual oil stoop on the side. A carved salamander winds around the stonework

a miniature alabaster effigy to Thomas Cockayne. Under his head is a helmet with a cock's head, a pun on the family name. The effigy is thought to be small because he died young in a brawl in 1488, before his father.

A tomb, from around the 13th century, in memory of Sir John Rossington, is also impressive, He lies cross legged, with a heart in his hands and his feet resting on a dog.

A small figure carving is found on the wall opposite the main entrance. It has been dated to the 12th century and could represent a pilgrim.

The east window is by Pre-Raphaelite artists Morris and Burne Jones.

# The Lantern Theatre

**Tucked away in a leafy road in Nether Edge is a small but perfectly formed theatre, rescued at the eleventh hour from the ravages of time...**

The Lantern Theatre before the later extensions were added

The Lantern Theatre is a tiny time capsule of Victorian days. With its half-timbered facade and red pan tiles, it is a delightful spot to visit and evoke the feeling of a bygone age, as well as enjoy a play in its intimate surroundings.

## Beginnings and decline

This little theatre, on Kenwood Park Road, was built in 1894 by a wealthy cutler, William Webster, who called it the Chalet Theatre. He entertained lavishly in his own home and had many actor friends coming up to stay from London. He designed the perfectly formed but tiny venue as a private 'toy' theatre for his daughters and for his guests to perform at. It was built on land adjoining the family home, next to their stable block and tennis courts.

There were no seats in the theatre, and when a play was put on. sofas and chairs would be brought across from the house. The audience would settle down, with a roaring coal fire to keep them warm in winter and wait for the show to begin.

By the 1950's the Webster family were long gone and the Chalet Theatre began its sad decline into an unloved ruin, with just a brief spell of activity in the 1920's when a dancing mistress used it for a while.

## A dream becomes reality

In the early 1940's and 50's, a local amateur theatrical group, run by a woman called Dilys Guite, was doing well, with three plays annually at the Library Theatre, Sheffield. Dilys was an actress and drama teacher from Birley Carr.

Her group used church halls for their rehearsals. Dilys had founded the theatre group in 1947 and was keen to find them a permanent home.

The account given by Dilys Guite as to how she found the theatre is a romantic drama in itself. She gave a reading about her discovery and eventual takeover of the then Chalet Theatre on the radio programme Woman's Hour...

One day she was wheeling her baby son in his pushchair down the leafy Kenwood Park Road in Nether Edge. She stopped to pick up a toy he had dropped and as she stood up, she saw the old neglected theatre in front of her.

*"It stood in small tangled shrubbery, surrounded by tall trees, with the front door creaking on broken hinges.... I was quite enchanted by it."*

Even so, Dilys let the moment go and put the experience to the back of her mind. Life took over and they moved 10 miles away, outside Sheffield.

## The Players get a new home

Fate took a hand six years later, however, when the family moved back to the city and ended up living just 200 yards away from the old building.

Dilys gazed at the neglected theatre each morning as she did the dishes until one day she decided to try and use the place. She made telephone enquiries and found the office of the owner was virtually next door to her. It all seemed meant to be. Within half an hour she had secured the keys and a deal to rent the place. That evening at six the players saw their new home.

> *"I too had always dreamed in a vague way of 'having a theatre' but there was a magical difference in the dream - it came true"* DILYS GUITE

It was owned at the time by a Mr Charles E Richardson, of The Nook, Millthorpe, a friendly octogenarian who had refused many offers to sell the theatre in the 30 years it had been derelict. He still had hopes it would be rebuilt and used as a theatre again. He was glad of the new interest and rented the theatre to the Dilys Guite Players for just £1 a week.

In May 1957, the group moved in. Sixteen or so actors and actresses, armed with tools, buckets, mops and bags of determination began to bring the old forgotten theatre back to life.

## Peeks at the Past

They had very little besides their enthusiasm. The work seemed almost impossible. The floor had dry rot and had collapsed, there was dust, cobwebs, broken windows with wooden battens, and on top of that it wad said to be haunted!. The cavity below the floorboards was filled with the accumulated debris of 30 years, including an old printing press, several hundred shoes, an old car body and two gas stoves. But the proscenium arch with its ornate plaster work was still perfect. The estimated cost for rebuilding at the time was a whopping £4,000.

Dilys, her architect husband and a man called Neville Simpkin, who later became Theatre Manager, set up a plan for restoration. It was decided the players would do as much work as possible themselves, using tradespeople for just the major plumbing and electrical work. An appeal was launched. A glossy, expensive brochure sent to leading representatives of industry only drew a guinea, but a cheaper appeal leaflet sent to smaller organisations and individuals got much more in the way of donations. The efforts captured people's imagination and many gave practical gifts of paint, concrete etc. Some tradespeople worked for reduced rates or free.

The work was hard and slow, but the company were given a terrific morale boost when owner Mr Richardson actually *gave* them the theatre in memory of his wife Annie.

### A new lease of life

Just six months later, in October 1957, the new theatre, now named the Lantern after the lantern dome on the roof, emerged from the dereliction, proudly decorated in grey and lime green, with blue velvet curtains on stage and a sparkling revamp of the outside. Seats had been added, with the theatre holding 95, including the tiny balcony seating just 19. When the players had taken on the theatre it was valued at just £700. At the time of an opening ceremony to celebrate the completion of the work, it was valued at £8,000.

The opening ceremony was on November 2, with the Lord and Lady Mayor in attendance and also a famous actor of the time, Jack Hulbert, as a guest. A short play, "The Dark Lady of the Sonnets" by George Bernard Shaw, was part of the evening.

The first full length play performed was The Merry Wives of Windsor, seven months to the day after the Dilys Guite Players had taken on the massive renovation task.

A Star photo of theatre interior, showing the proscenium arch

The facilities still left something to be desired, with the actors having to dash between changing rooms in the stableblock across the yard to the theatre. Refreshments consisted of a large tea urn, ferried from the house of a dedicated member three miles away!

In 1962 the theatre had its first redecoration. The aim was for a Victorian feel and the pale blue walls had a Victorian motif, with a dark blue ceiling and cherry red curtains. Most of the cost was covered by donations.

At the Lantern Theatre's first birthday, a dinner dance was held at the S&E Arcade restaurant on Ecclesall Road. It was on Thursday 17 April and tickets cost 10/6 (about 53p). The entertainment was by Fred Jubb and his band.

The programmes of the theatre became collector's pieces, with fine drawings by one of the Dilys Guite Players' members, a designer called Anthony Webb, who had trained at the Sheffield College of Art.

Above, Figure of Fun, André Roussin, (13-18 April 1964), and right, The Provok'd Wife, Sir John Vanbrugh (Nov 26-Dec 1 1962)

### The theatre today

A foyer extension and a coffee lounge/bar area were later added. The theatre is now Grade II listed, as well as a registered charity. The Dilys Guite Players still own the place and are members of the Sheffield and District Amateur Theatre Association, putting on several shows and events a year.

The theatre is available for hire. Call 0114 2551776 for details.

# Bishop's House

**Tucked away in one of Sheffield's parks is a lovely old timber framed house...**

I n the Norton Lees area of the city, at the top of Meersbrook Park, stands the best preserved and earliest example of a timber-framed house to have survived in Sheffield.

## The beginnings

At the time the house was built, the area, now with houses clustered around the park, would have been fields, with the odd farm or hamlet dotted about. There would also have been an up and coming industry of scythe-making. No one knows who Bishop's House was built for, but it was begun around 1500.

It was most likely built as a small manor house for minor gentry, or as a large farmhouse for a prosperous yeoman (someone who owned his own land). This first house was framed completely of timber, which was a relatively common and cheaper way of building then. Stone did not become more common until the end of the 16th century at least, when oak became scarce. The oak timber was cut and shaped to size, then it was provisionally fitted together and all the pieces numbered. This meant they could be moved to the house site and re-assembled like a giant jigsaw. Some markings, believed to be an old numbering system, (short dashes based on Roman numerals) can still be seen on one of the wall timbers.

## Home comforts...

The house was once smaller, with a hall, a kitchen and private family rooms. The hall was the main focus of the house. In poorer homes, it was used for cooking, eating and sleeping.

At this time buildings were usually only one room wide, because they had problems putting a roof on anything wider. Any extra rooms were added as cross wings, a little like playing dominoes! The building had no fireplaces then, they were added much later. Oak latticework windows, or mullions in the wall were open to the elements, providing light and letting out smoke from the fire. They also had wooden shutters to stop draughts. The first floor mullioned window in the east gable is oldest.

When the timber frame of the house was assembled, the gaps in the wood skeleton were filled in to complete the walls.

Wattle and daub is the best known method, but in the Sheffield area stone slates inserted between timbers and covered in plaster were often used. At Bishops House, however, plaster over thin pieces of oak (laths) was used. Locally quarried stone slates were used for the roof, with any gaps being stuffed with sphagnum moss to keep out the weather.

The characteristic black and white stripey look of the house is not original, as the wood was not painted, but left as natural oak. Blackening the timbers with tar was sometimes carried out, but not everywhere.

## Why the name Bishop's House?

There is a local tradition that two brothers of a family by the name of Blythe lived in the house in their youth, later both becoming Bishops. John Blythe was Bishop of Salisbury from 1494 to 1499 and Geoffrey was Bishop of Lichfield and Coventry from 1503 to 1533.

There is no evidence to support this story, however, and the house is not thought to be old enough for them to have lived there then. Also such a well off family would probably have had a much larger house.

Peeks at the Past

## William Blythe

The earliest occupant of Bishop's House there is evidence for is William Blythe, who lived there in 1627. He was responsible for a lot of the 'home improvements' there.

His initials also appear on the wood wall panelling in the hall.

He was descended from a different branch of the family than the two brothers and left many details of his life behind, showing he was a farmer and perhaps the largest local producer of scythes before the Civil War.

A farmer sharpens his scythe

When he died in 1631, an inventory of his possessions was made and provides details of the house and the extent of his wealth. Items included 77 items of pewter, 25 items of brassware and some silverware.

Outhouses then in place around the house but now gone were listed as a kiln, a bakehouse, a wainhouse (for six wagons), a stable and a servants' parlour.

He was also renting equipment to grinders and smiths who were working for him, showing he practiced dual professions of both farmer and industrialist.

## The Civil War and decline

During the Civil war, from 1642 to 1646, little building was carried out anywhere. It was only after the war that his son, another William, carried out more work on Bishop's House, including a stone extension, decorative plasterwork and replacing some of the decayed timbers with stone infill.

Apart from his own building aspirations, he was also good at demolition, being a Parliamentarian and one of two local officers responsible for organising the destruction of Sheffield Castle in 1648.

He even bought bits of it, paying £3 for 'bords and plaster' possibly re-used in his improvements at Bishop's House. He died in 1665 and his gravestone can be seen in the porch of Norton Parish Church.

The last Blythe to live in the house was Samuel, a minister at Attercliffe. After he died the property was sold.

The house declined, being let to a tenant farmer and his labourer and made into separate dwellings.

A new staircase, a dairy, new windows, partitions and fireplaces were added, but the house maintains most of its 17th century form.

## Restoration & the museum

In 1886 the property was given to the Corporation when Meersbrook Park was formed. Restoration work was carried out and outbuildings were demolished. There were no major alterations until 1974, when the house was lived in by families of Recreation Department employees. In July 1976, after extensive restoration, the house was opened as a museum. All furniture is based upon inventories - only the panelling survived the years.

## Ghostly Goings On...

As with any old property, there are tales of ghosts at Bishop's House. A tall woman in white has been spotted walking through the gardens. Not too unusual - except that she carried on walking - straight through the wall!

Some people believe she is Mary Blythe, who lived there in the 17th century.

Also at the house is a mysterious haunted box in the bedroom. This old trinket box, made around 1600, is empty but kept locked, with the key stored at Weston Park Museum. Even so, some mornings it is found unlocked with its lid lifted back when no one has touched it...

*Bishop's House is on Norton Lees Lane, Sheffield S8 9BE. Signposted from the A61 Sheffield to Chesterfield Road. Buses 33, 34 and 25 from High Street in the city centre stop nearby. School parties are welcome and freelance educators in costume are available. Pre-booked groups only during week.*
***Open:** Saturday 10 - 4.30pm and Sunday, 11 - 4.30pm.*
***Admission free.***
*For further information ring **(0114) 2557701** during opening hours.*

Below: A Whitsuntide Parade along Brook Road, with Meersbrook Park on the left

PHOTO: STAR NEWSPAPER ARCHIVES

## The Ruskin Museum

Set within the grounds of the park is old Meersbrook Hall. Once a private residence it was a splendid place, with peacocks wandering the grounds. When the park was made it had become derelict, but was renovated to become a museum to house the art objects collected by John Ruskin. Ruskin was a writer, artist and critic. He wanted to bring art to the common man and open a gallery. He chose Sheffield for this as the contrast of ugly industrialisation and beautiful surroundings fascinated him. He also admired the city's many skilled craftspeople, and founded The Guild of St. George in 1871, to oversee his projects. Ruskin's first gallery opened in 1875, at a cottage in Bell Hagg Road, Walkley, but rapidly outgrew the building. From there it was transferred to Meersbrook Hall in 1890, which became known as the Ruskin Museum.

Photo:
Star Archives

The collection included watercolours, drawings, minerals, prints and plaster casts, intended to be used as an educational resource.

During the war years, the museum closed due to diminished interest, and the collection went into storage.

It was not until the early 1980's that the collection appeared again, when a new Ruskin gallery was opened in a former wine shop on Norfolk Street and became a popular and award winning attraction.

This Ruskin Gallery later closed and the collection is now based in the new Millennium Galleries in Sheffield City Centre. Pawson and Brailsford's Guide of 1879 lists the museum, then in full swing in the Walkey site, as an earlier tourist attraction.

*"This unique and interesting museum, founded by Mr John Ruskin, the eminent writer and art critic, is at Upper Walkley...Mr Ruskin purchased an acre of land with a good stone cottage upon it several years ago and uses the principal room in the cottage for the museum. ... The contents of the museum at present are: 1, A small but rich and rare mineral collection, containing some of the finest specimens of precious stone the country possesses. Probably nowhere else in Europe can so valuable a collection be found in so small a space. 2. A natural history section, composed not of stuffed specimens out of which all the life has gone, but of the best illustrated works published...3. A botany section, composed of carefully executed drawings, some of the most beautiful being Mr Ruskin's own work. 4. A small collection of paintings and drawings, chiefly from the old masters...5. A small collection of classical literature....There are also a few busts and other studies"*

PHOTO: STAR NEWSPAPER ARCHIVES

Views inside the old Ruskin Museum

Old Ruskin Museum in Meersbrook Park

PHOTO: FROM AN OLD POSTCARD

## Meersbrook Park

The fountain near the old Ruskin Museum was erected in 1891 'by members of the British United Order of Oddfellows to perpetuate the memory of William Westran one of the founders and corresponding secretary for twenty one years. He died while in office April 2nd 1889 in his 66th year'.

The Corporation acquired land in 1886 to begin this park. The trend at the time was to build places for the 'constitutional walks' then popular. Meersbrook means 'the brook of the meadow'. It became a splendid park, much bigger than it is now and stretched over what is now rows of housing.

There was once a rosary and a pond with water lilies.

Present facilities include 2 tennis courts, bowling greens and a playground. There are entrances in Brook Road, Meersbrook Park Road and Norton Lees Lane. From the top of the park there is a splendid view over the city. In winter snow, the sloping grass banks are much loved by sledgers.

# St Marie's Cathedral

On Norfolk Row, squeezed in between shops and banks, stands a stunning example of Gothic Revival architecture in the form of Sheffield's Catholic Cathedral...

St. Maries Cathedral is an aesthetic surprise for anyone cutting down Norfolk Row from busy Fargate.

### Secret Catholisism

Until 1559, Catholics worshipped at the medieval parish church of St Peter and Paul (now the Anglican Cathedral) and at the Chapel of our Lady, on what is still called Lady's Bridge.

After this date the Catholic faith became outlawed by Royal Decree and the Anglican Book of Prayer became the norm. Attendance at services was compulsory and those who did not do so were fined and put on a register. This, together with the lack of Catholic clergy, meant that most people conformed.

During the 16th, 17th and 18th centuries the threat to the catholic faith continued. It was safer to be in the countryside to attend secret masses than it was in the towns. Many people hid priests in their houses at great risk, in 'priest holes'. Codes were devised to indicate mass being perfomed, such as spreading a white sheet on a bush outside the house. Catholic priests from Padley Hall, near Grindleford, were caught in 1588 and taken to Derby to be executed. The men, Robert Ludlam and Nicolas Garlick, became known as the Padley Martyrs.

In 1701, Thomas Duke of Norfolk was a Catholic living in Sheffield. He had an agent called John Shireburn, who lived on Coal Pit Lane (now Cambridge Street). Thomas decided to build a house with a secret chapel, as building Catholic chapels was still illegal . He moved John into a specially built residence on the corner of Norfolk Row, just off Fargate, which became known as The Lord's House. The chapel was in the roof, measured 50ft x 28ft and held 600 people.

By 1791, many of the restrictions on Catholism had been lifted and it was possible to build Catholic churches.

Attendance grew and by 1814, the Lord's House was too small. Money was raised by the congregation to build a bigger chapel. This was finished two years later, in May 1816.

Angel statue given to St Marie's in 1930, in memory of John Bernasconi

It stood back from Norfolk Row. In between the building and Norfolk Row itself was a Catholic graveyard. (Some stones from this are built into the wall of St Marie's).

The priest of the new chapel was Father Richard Rimmer. After him, various priests resided. In 1843 a Father Joseph Pratt took over and was very enthusiastic. He acquired the land next to the chapel for £1,400 and had a scheme to build a bigger, better church. This began in 1847, when the chapel was demolished and the land preparation started.

The cornerstone of the new church was laid by Bishop Briggs on March 25 of the same year. The main architect was a man called Ellison Hadfield, from the same firm that built the cholera monument.

Later, in 1849, the old graveyard was moved to St Bede's church in Rotherham. In February of that year, as the church was well underway, Father Pratt died. Some say he caught a chill when he was helping to move bodies from the Catholic Graveyard over to St Bede's. He was also buried at St Bede's, but the stonemason, Benjamin Gregory, who was working on the new church knew he would have rather been interred in this new church. Benjamin built Father Pratt a tomb in the church and on the night of March 24, he went to St Bede's, took Fr. Pratt's body and put it to rest in the tomb he had prepared for him at St. Marie's.

This painted figure from the exterior of the cathedral is St Joseph. The statue once stood inside in St Joseph's chapel

## Peeks at the Past

When the church opened, an effigy of Fr Pratt was also made above the tomb. It is in the mortuary chapel and shows the priest holding his partly finished church. At his shoulder sits an angel and his feet rest upon a dog. Nearby is a pillar which has some beautiful angels carved around it.

St Marie's became the Catholic Cathedral for this city in 1980, when the new Hallam Diocese was created.

This crowned head is at the left of the Norfolk Row entrance

### OTHER FEATURES IN ST MARIE'S

By each of the doors is a *piscina,* for holding holy water. People entering the church can use this to bless themselves as they go through the entrance.

Also around the walls are lovely stations of the cross and some elaborate candleholder's. In St Josephs chapel are painted tiles showing nuns of Notre Dame who came to Sheffield in 1855 to help with the schools in the town.

The names of two priests (Robert Ludlam and Nicholas Garlick) captured at Padley Chapel and later martyred at Derby are among names painted on the wall above the sanctuary.

The West Window, at the back of the cathedral, has a lovely image of the story of Jonah and the whale. The East window tells the story of the life of the Virgin Mary.

On the Nave roof are coats of arms in the form of shields. First is that of Thomas More, one time Lord Chancellor of England, second is of John Fisher, one time Bishop of Rochester and the third is of Philip Howard, one time Earl of Norfolk.

On the rectory of St. Marie's, over the door to the sacristy, is an elaborate figure scene. This is the Annunciation, when Mary is told by the angel Gabriel that she is with child. It was carved by the artist Thomas Earp, in 1879. He also sculpted the 'Atlantes' statues on Bryward House on Commercial Street in 1874. The scene is in a niche with an ornate canopy.

### SERVICES AT ST MARIE'S

**Sunday Mass**
Saturday 6.30
Sunday 8.30 10.30 6.30
Mass in Polish 12.30
10am morning prayer

**Weekday Masses**
Mon - Fri 8am 12.45, Saturday 12.30

Telephone 0114 272 2522
e mail: smariecathedral@aol.com
www.stmariecathedral-sheffield.org

Effigy of Father Pratt in the Mortuary Chapel

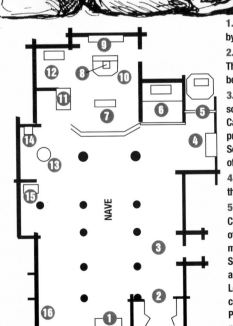

1. West window, designed by Pugin.

2. Reconciliation room. The door leads to the bellringing chamber above.

3. SOUTH TRANSEPT with some gravestones from a Catholic cemetery, previously on this site. South window and statue of St. Patrick.

4. SOUTH AISLE stations of the cross begin.

5. Up the stairs is the Lady Chapel. The marble statue of the Virgin Mary was made in Rome. The altar is Sicilian marble. The pillars are from the Pyrenees. Look back at the window commemorating the Padley Martyrs, Catholic priests from Padley Hall who were martyred.

6. ST JOSEPH'S or NORFOLK CHAPEL. The altar piece shows St Joseph on his deathbed with Jesus showing his place in heaven. The floor is decorated with emblems of the Duke of Norfolk.

7. The SANCTUARY. The central altar is the focal point of the church. The bishop's seat or *cathedra* is nearby.
This is where the name *Cathedral* comes from.

8. Carved stone from original altar.

9. The East Window. It shows Mary clothed in the sun, standing on the moon and crowned with seven stars. The other pictures are scenes from her life.

10. The SEDILIA or seat for the clergy.

11. The organ. It has 1700 pipes. Between the organ and the wall is the resting place of Fr. Pratt, who began this church building.

12. BLESSED SACRAMENT CHAPEL. The modern windows represent the sacraments of baptism and confirmation

13. The FONT. The glass tile nearby gives light to the crypt.

14. The Shrine of Our Lady. The statue is made of limewood. Mary's emblem of the Fleurs de Lys (iris) is included in the design.

15. The Mortuary Chapel. Under the altar is an effigy of Fr. Pratt holding the almost complete church, which was still being built when he died.

16. The Martyr's window.

## Carvings around Fargate

The book, pens and quills (right) can be found on a building opposite Chapel Walk. There is a carving of a second book, with candles and spectacles, the date 1879 and an eagle holding oak branches. At the top of ornate pillars are two birds and two rat like creatures.

The broody, bearded head below is on a building just to the left of the old jennel known as Black Swan Walk. At the apex are two gryphons, the date 1897 and other carved heads and decorations which abound on this ornate frontage.

On what was once a YMCA building, almost opposite Orchard Square and near Norfolk Row, are a series of carvings showing THE CREATION. They begin with God, (represented by a triangle), then the heavens (shown above), mountains, sea creatures (left) and Adam and Eve.

Above WH Smith are carved four animal heads, from an earlier use of the shop

### Old Albany Hotel

On Surrey Street and opposite Orchard Square is a lovely old building that was once the Albany Hotel. Chained lions parade across a freize, whilst shield bearing figures and sad looking winged dragons decorate the rest.

## Chapel Walk

Chapel Walk, just off the busy Fargate Shopping Precinct is still like an old medieval street in feel, because of the narrow path and shops, still sticking to the old layout.

This lovely carved name sign is all that remains of a gallery that must have once been a popular spot on the busy thoroughfare.

The signs over the entrance to Chapel Walk are by an artist named Andrew Bell. They are made of painted metal and were placed there in 1996.

16

# Padley Chapel

In the picturesque Padley Gorge by a popular walking spot are the remains of an old hall, with its restored chapel, and tales of religious struggle and martyrdom...

Padley Gorge, near the village of Grindleford. is home to Padley Chapel, built on the first floor of the gatehouse of a grand manor house which once stood here.

### The Eyres

In the 16th century Padley Hall, (built in the 14th century), was home to the Eyre family. The last of the Padley Eyres died in 1560, and his daughter Anne inherited the hall and lands.

She married Sir Thomas Fitzherbert of Norbury. He was a staunch Catholic and Catholic priests often visited the hall. At the time, Queen Elizabeth I was on the throne, and the religion of the country was that of the Protestant faith. It was illegal to be a Catholic priest, with any found practising tried for treason. Anyone found to be harbouring a priest was also commiting an offence and tried for this crime.

Thomas Fitzherbert, living in Norbury with Anne, was imprisoned for his faith in 1561. His brother John was tenant at Padley Hall. Any priestly visits there had to be in secret. They were careful but John Fitzherbert was still suspected of Catholic worship and on July 12th, 1588, the Earl of Shrewsbury sent men to the Hall to arrest him. Two Catholic priests, Nicholas Garlick and Robert Ludlam, were also found there and arrested.

Nicholas Garlick, born in 1555, was from near Glossop, and after time at college returned to Derbyshire to take over the free school at Tideswell. In 1581 he went abroad to study at the college in Rheims, France. After his ordination in 1582 he returned to England. There were spies at the time watching the movements of any Catholic priests and he was found, arrested and deported back to Rheims. He decided to risk returning to England, however, and Padley was one of the places he came to say mass.

*The chapel on the bridge at Derby*

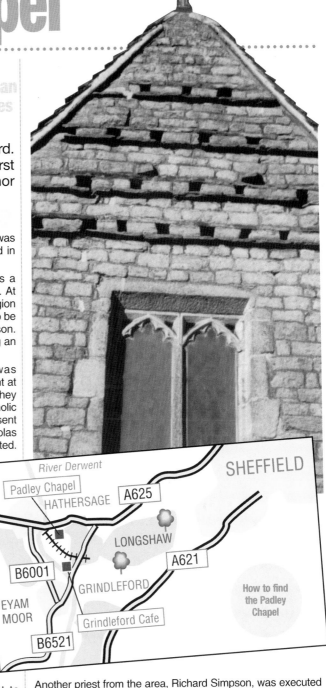

Robert Ludlam had studied at St John's College, Oxford. In 1580 he too went to study at Rheims. He was ordained in 1581. The year after he returned to England. His movements after that are unknown until his arrest at Padley.

After being captured at Padley, the priests were taken off for trial. Their gruesome end was to be hung, drawn and quartered, with their heads then being impaled on spikes on the old St Mary's Bridge in Derby, by the bridge chapel.*

Another priest from the area, Richard Simpson, was executed at the same time. John Fitzherbert was imprisoned for harbouring the priests and died in captivity.

The hall fell into ruin. The gatehouse was used as a cowshed to a farm, which meant that it was preserved a little better. The 14th century wooden roof, built in a style known as 'hammerbeam' still survives. The foundations of the old hall can be seen at the back of the chapel, including remains of a spiral staircase.

A pilgrimage is made to the chapel every year, on the Sunday nearest 12th July, in memory of the priests who died for their faith, and were later known as the Padley Martyrs. The chapel is usually open on Wednesdays and Sundays, 2pm to 4pm, April to September.

* This 14th century chapel is still there, one of only five complete bridge chapels still standing in the country. The tiny building, just 45ft long by 14ft wide, was restored in 1930. It now houses some lovely modern stained glass.

## Around Padley Chapel

### Grindleford

This pretty village lies near Padley Gorge and just 10 miles from the centre of Sheffield. It is in the east side of the Peak District National Park in the valley of the major river, the Derwent. The name is from the former industry of grindstone quarrying and the fact that it has long been a river crossing location. There is a lovely old 3 star hotel called the Maynard Arms, as well as the climbers' and walkers' favourite haunt, the Grindleford Cafe. This is housed in the old Victorian station building, which was built in 1898, extended in 1925 and closed in 1965 during Beeching's cutbacks. An old wooden ticket barrier is still there, as is an old station clock. It is a great place for chip butties!

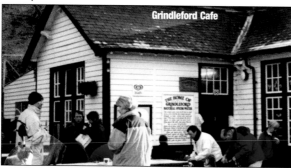

Grindleford Cafe

### Longshaw

This area, now belonging to the national trust, is a popular spot for walkers. The area was once a shooting estate of the Duke of Rutland. There are 1,700 acres of woodland and moorland to explore, and also a shop, Lodge cafe and information centre. Sheep Dog trials are held here in early September.

Padley Chapel

### Flycatchers

Padley Gorge is home to Pied Flycatchers, a stout bird with a small bill. They are around 12-13cm (4-5ins) tall. The male has white in the wing and on the forehead. The female is brown with a smaller white area in the wing. They live in woods and perch openly, looking for passing insects.

### Totley Tunnel

By the side of the cafe is the opening of this impressive Tunnel, built between 1888 and 1893. At 3.5 miles long it is said to be the second longest in Britain. (The longest is said to be the Severn Tunnel). It passes under moorland and took the labour of 100's of navvies.

PHOTO: THE STAR ARCHIVES

18

# Carbrook Hall

**By the side of busy Attercliffe common is an old pub that was once owned by an officer in Oliver Cromwell's army...**

This popular pub on Attercliffe Common was once the home of the Lord of the Manor of Ecclesall, Thomas Bright, in the days of Queen Elizabeth the First.

### Origins of the old hall

The original hall that has partly survived as the Carbrook Hall public house was built in the late half of the 15th century. It was before that a timber framed house, said to date back to the 12th century, when it was the home of the Blunt family. Once it was much larger. The wing now surviving as a pub was added in 1620. The dates could be mixed up with another older building which used to stand nearby, however. The building as we see it today dates back from at least the 1460's. The Lord of the Manor of Ecclesall, Thomas Bright. once lived here. The name of the area - Brightside - comes from the Bright family name and the name Meadowhall probably refers to the meadows by this old hall.

By 1637 the hall was owned by a later member of the Bright family, Colonel John Bright, who was in Oliver Cromwell's army in the English Civil War (1642-1649). He was appointed governor of Sheffield Castle after the Roundheads had taken it from Royal control in 1644. He died in 1688 and the Carbrook estate passed through families called Thompson and Whetham, until it came to an Admiral Frank Sotheron, His sister sold half of it. In the 19th century the old hall became a public house.

### The Oak Room

This is a lovely wood panelled room, which still has the original door and walls over two feet thick. This is a splendid example of a Jacobean interior, with dark oak panels on the walls and plaster frieze and ceiling. The ceiling bears ornate patterns, with flowers scrolls and lots of thistle motifs.

The mantlepiece is the main focus, however. The centrepiece of this wooden surround has a man standing on a prostate horned devil type figure. This represents wisdom (the man) trampling out ignorance (the horned beast figure). Scrolls carved around the figures say:

*"Good understanding is to depart from evil. Be not as a horse or a mule which have no understanding. Understanding reacheth Heaven. Understanding is a well-spring of life. Ignorance is a beast."*

There are also two pillars carved with shields and flowers.

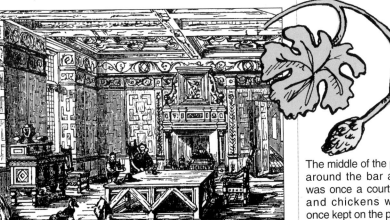

An old print of the interior of Carbrook Hall

The middle of the pub, around the bar area was once a courtyard and chickens were once kept on the piece of ground now used as a carpark.

The mantelpiece in the Oak Room and a detail of wisdom trampling on ignorance

Peeks at the Past

### The Dark Oak Room

This room is not open to the public as it is part of the landlord's accommodation. It is similar oak panelling the Oak Room downstairs. A carving on this fireplace shows a bird hunting a worm. There are also some small Elizabethan style heads carved as decoration.

### The Brewhouse and Kitchens

In the pool room are to be found the old hall ovens. Here grand dishes would be cooked and ale would be brewed. The one on the right still has the old cooking black pot. Red lights placed in the ovens help to recreate the old kitchen atmosphere.

### The most haunted public house?

Carbrook Hall is said to be the most haunted pub in Sheffield. A visiting psychic said most of the spirits are in the brewhouse area and are harmless, but one troublesome spirit is 'banished into the wall' to the right of the bar. Funnily enough this is where bottles have mysteriously hurled themselves from the drink chiller cabinet, to fly over landlord Phil Skelton's shoulder. Phil himself has seen many unexplained things, such as a man in old style uniform on the stairs and figures walking into the pool room that then disappear. It is said there is a tunnel from the pub to Manor Castle. Though it is hard to tell as the cellar is now blocked, but many older locals say that they can remember being shown a tunnel here when they were young children.

The pub sign, plus ghost boasts

The Oak Room ceiling

Does the ghost of John Bright, still walk around his old home? Perhaps...

This is an image of John Bright from a stained glass window in the organ chamber of **Sheffield Anglican Cathedral.** **The glass is by Christopher Webb and was** given by Mary Newton Firth in 1938, in memory **of her husband** Bernard and her son Alec. The Bright coat of arms, in the form of a shield, is shown above the figure.

Below: The old ovens, complete with an old cooking pot

e mail: info@carbrookhall.co.uk  website: www. carbrookhall.co.uk Telephone number: 0114 2440117

# Old Queen's Head

**Tucked away near the hustle and bustle of the bus and rail stations in the centre of Sheffield is an ancient old timbered building, enjoying life as a historic pub...**

Just by the Transport Interchange at Pond Street, not far from the Midland Railway Station, nestles a remnant of the past. The Old Queen's Head Inn is said by some to be named after Mary Queen of Scots, in whose era the building began its life, though this name has always been popular for public houses.

## The Hall in the Ponds

The building was originally a hall, probably built by the Earl of Shrewsbury in the late 15th century. It was part of Sheffield Castle estate and is said to be the oldest domestic building in Sheffield.

The Ponds was the name given to the flat marshy area alongside the River Sheaf. Here would be ponds that would probably be stocked with fish to feed the castle, as well as a water supply to power the local corn mill. Thus the building became known as 'the hall in the ponds'.

In the 19th century it was said the old hall was the laundry of the castle, but it is much too grand to be such a lowly building. It is more likely to be a lodge that the gentry out hunting in the park then covering the area would take refreshment in. Old plans show that the hall was once larger, and an L-shape. The frames of these timber buildings were made of oak.

The oak was cut and used whilst still green and unseasoned. When the wood dried out it would often buckle, which is why many of these old houses look so crooked.

Below, an old print of the pub and right, as it looks today. Above are some of the wood carvings from the beams.

The wooden pieces would be put together on site, then the spaces were infilled with lath and plaster and a roof of stone slabs added.

Fine carvings are to be found on the exterior and over the bar. The ones on the exterior are said to represent the sixth Earl of Shrewsbury and Bess of Hardwick, his wife, who built Hardwick Hall. One carving over the bar is of a queen's head, which could be another explanation for the name given to this old alehouse.

In the mid nineteenth century a man called James Pilley, who was a nailmaker, bought a licence to turn the building into an ale house and called it The Old Queen's Head. Trade grew more and more brisk and the pub was passed to various owners, eventually being taken over by the council, who leased it to John Smiths of Tadcaster.

*Above is a photograph of the queen's head from over the bar*

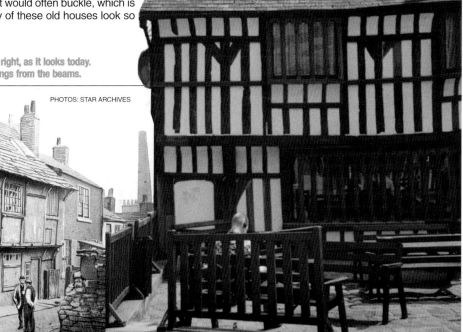

PHOTOS: STAR ARCHIVES

Peeks at the Past

## Renovation

Extensive work was carried out in 1949, when the original timbers were revealed by removing years worth of plaster and whitewash.

An old stone fireplace and two windows were discovered, as well as a more modern cast iron fireplace and a filled-in well shaft. Two clay pipes were also found in the chimney.

## Ghostly guest

The ghost of Mary Queen of Scots is said to haunt the aptly named pub. Mary was beheaded in 1587 in the great Hall at Fotheringay Castle near Peterborough. She was 44. She spent 13 years and nine months in the Sheffield district, at Sheffield Castle, Sheffield Manor Lodge and also at the house at Chatsworth.

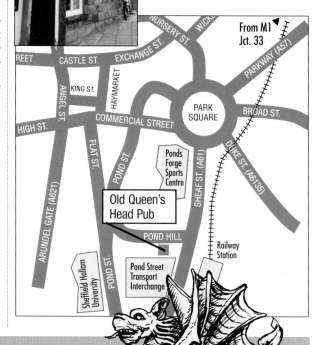

The pub was renovated again in 1993. and extended and altered, with new windows and external seating areas.

It is a tenancy now, serving various brews.

Telephone (0114) 2798383 for details of opening hours

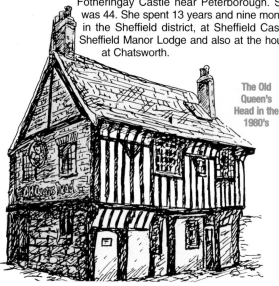

The Old Queen's Head in the 1980's

## Sheffield Midland Railway Station

This dragon/serpent creature, called a wyvern. is carved on the front of the station. It is a symbol of the old railway company

The busy rail terminus for Sheffield, on the old Midland Line, was completed in 1905. Rail travel was becoming more and more popular and the station already built there in 1870 was too small. Victoria Station, now closed, near the Wicker, was also serving Sheffield, but still was not sufficient.

The Midland Station was designed by architect Charles Trubshawe. When it was opened it drew criticism for being too low in appearance and because it did not have a tower, as many others of the time did. The Sheffield Telegraph called it 'a splendid opportunity lost'.

The front of the station had a 300ft awning at the front, to shelter cabs, luggage and passengers arriving and departing.

The new building had two new platforms, 3 and 4, added. The old frontage from the building before became Platform 2 and a new platform 1 was built.

At the time of writing there are plans in the pipeline to revamp the station area.

The station exterior in 1895, before the improvements

PHOTOS: STAR ARCHIVES

After improvements in 1905

# Old Banners Store

**The white edifice of one of Sheffield's oldest stores brings back memories for many people**

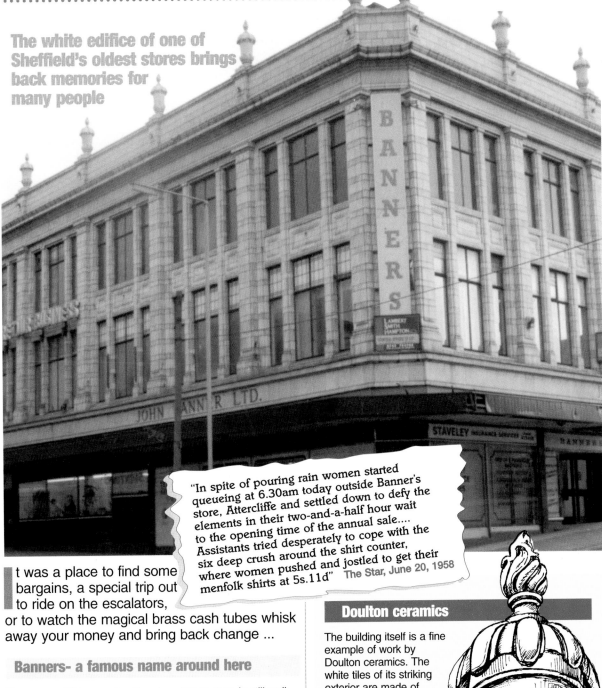

"In spite of pouring rain women started queueing at 6.30am today outside Banner's store, Attercliffe and settled down to defy the elements in their two-and-a-half hour wait to the opening time of the annual sale.... Assistants tried desperately to cope with the six deep crush around the shirt counter, where women pushed and jostled to get their menfolk shirts at 5s.11d" *The Star, June 20, 1958*

It was a place to find some bargains, a special trip out to ride on the escalators, or to watch the magical brass cash tubes whisk away your money and bring back change ...

### Banners- a famous name around here

The name of this once bustling department store is still well known, associated with the huge old white building in Attercliffe, topped with rows of decorative ceramic urns. Many people remember the fact that it was the first store outside London to use escalators.

The place was founded in the late 1800's by a man called John Banner, but the present building dates from the 1930's. The store's proud slogan was:

### "Bargains are our business"

It became a great local institution. Many children would come here to buy their new Whitsuntide clothes and shoes. The store had a credit system using they own money tokens or cheques. It also had a tube system for sending money through the store.

### Doulton ceramics

The building itself is a fine example of work by Doulton ceramics. The white tiles of its striking exterior are made of Carraraware. The name comes from the fact that its white crystalline glaze made it look similar to Carrara marble from Italy. The material was first used for vases, but later for architectural work. It was often used in different colours on cinemas. The urns are by the artist FW Pomeroy.

## Peeks at the Past

Money or cheques would be put into a little container which was placed into the tube and pressure shot it up the tube to the cashier department.
Receipts or change came back the same way.

### End of an era

This great store closed in January 1980, after 106 years of trading; only 11 of 91 employees were left by then.

For the mostly women staff, many of whom had worked there all their lives, the death of the store after 106 years meant much more than just the loss of a job. Many had been friends for years, leaving only to have a baby or join the forces and then come back to their job again.

The store director, Trevor Barter, closed the store a day earlier than expected, on Friday instead of Saturday, but the staff still wanted to go in for the emotional final day.

The store has since had various incarnations and today houses businesses, an antiques centre, a holiday shop, other small shops and The Courtyard Cafe.

"I thought it would help if they could get their tears over in half an hour, otherwise they would have spent all the Saturday crying. I just sprang it on them. We have all been dreading the last day and it seemed the best way to cope with it"
**Trevor Barter, The Star January 28, 1980**

"Slightly macabre groups of plastic mannequins, their wigs slipped over one eye and their arms stuck in unlikely attitudes, were the only witnesses to the quiet bustle of staff doing their final duties on Saturday"
**The Star January 28, 1980**

# Around Banners

## Attercliffe

The name comes from 'at the cliffe' at the bend in the River Don. Even up until the 1800's it was a pleasant country village. It was a rival shopping haunt to Sheffield city centre. Today there are many improvements to the Don Valley, including the Stadium, the Arena and entertainments, as well as a mixture of shops and pubs.

## Salmon Pastures

Nearby is an area known as Salmon Pastures. This was a fishing spot rich in salmon, as the name suggests, until the 18th century. It became polluted by industrial waste over the years and all the fish disappeared, but now it has greatly improved and is part of the lovely Five Weirs' Walk.The old name stone from the school can be seen set on the bank by the side of the canal.

Broughton Lane, not far away, is thought by many to be named after a notorious highwayman called Spence Broughton, who held up a mail coach in 1791.

He was sentenced to death and his body hung rotting in chains for many years from a gibbet. Now there is a pub called the Noose and Gibbet on the Lane, which has a replica body hanging outside.

## Washford Bridge

This place has been a passing point over the river for over 400 years. The earliest bridge was timber and stood a little upstream. In 1647 the bridge was the scene of a Civil War battle. The first stone bridge on this site was built in 1672.

In 1751 a toll road was built from Sheffield to Tinsley, which later became the Attercliffe Road. The present bridge was first built in 1795 and later widened in 1880. There are 'snow gates' on it, large gates where snow was pushed from the road into the river to clear the road. The five weirs' walk crosses here.

## Zeppelin raid

On Effingham Road. not far from Banners, is a stone wall memorial marking a sad event from the First World War, when a German zeppelin in an air raid dropped a bomb on the spot.
On this site on 26th September 1916, nine men, ten women and ten children died.

# Cholera monument

Near the Midland Railway Station, atop a grassy mound, is a broken Victorian tower commemorating over 400 victims of a deadly outbreak of Cholera...

It was in July of the year 1832 that the first cases of Cholera were claiming victims in Sheffield. The city was then only a market town with a population of just under 92,000, it was still relatively isolated and had escaped earlier outbreaks of the disease.

### A deadly foe

Cholera is a disease caused by the bacteria Vibrio Cholerae, which contaminates drinking water and food. It is still present today in many countries where the standard of hygiene is inadequate. Most cases now are mild, but the epidemic that swept Sheffield caused acute symptoms of muscle cramps, thirst, diarrhoea and vomiting. Severe dehydration caused death within three to four hours. At the time it was thought that the disease was spread in the air. In fact it is spread by an infected person contaminating food or water and can only be passed by human excrement, an indication of the unsanitary living conditions. An outbreak in Bengal spread to Europe and disease came to this country from ships entering the port of Sunderland in 1831. The first case was reported in October 1831. The disease soon got a grip in the towns, where poor working and living conditions made an ideal breeding ground. Cesspools and filth contaminated water in the poorer parts of the city and cholera was at first thought to afflict only the poor. This was soon disproved. Anyone drinking contaminated water caught it, whatever their social standing. People began to implement new guidelines to try and halt the epidemic. In London the Prevention of Cholera Act was passed in February 1832. Health Boards were set up in the various cities, including Sheffield. Recommendations in the London Board of Health reports give a glimpse of the conditions and lack of medical understanding at the time:

"Maintain personal cleanliness by frequent washing and change of clothing and, if available by occasional warm bathing...Let the diet consist of plain meats, bread and boiled vegetables, rejecting as injurious indigestible kinds of food, such as salads, raw fruits, nuts, rich pastry and such articles as an individual may have found to cause acidity, flatulence and indigestion."

"The Board of Health have recommended that internments of persons who have died of Cholera Morbus should be confined to the Church Yards of St. Philip's, St. Mark's and St. George's Churches and of Attercliffe and Ecclesall, but that none should take place in the other Church Yards and the interior of the town."

Sheffield escaped until July 1832. The city was expanding fast, with people coming to work in the area from the countryside. Cramped back to backs, open sewers and the practice of keeping livestock in residential areas made it a breeding ground for disease.

When the first Cholera victims died, they were buried in carefully chosen graveyards to try and keep the infection under control, but it didn't work and the death rate rose. Master Cutler, John Blake, died, proving that cholera did not only affect the drunk and idle, the poor and dirty. Specific graveyards were designated for the victims. In the newspaper at the time, The Iris, the public notice (left) appeared on July 24, 1832.

As more people died, the designated graveyards were full and by August an alternative had to be found. People wanted to bury the dead in an area that was isolated. The 12th Duke of Norfolk, Bernard Edwards, offered some of his land, in Sheffield Park (now Norfolk Park), which was then fairly isolated.

The monument complete, before it was damaged in gales

**Below: The monument today, shortened due to damage from the gales. There is a fine view over the city from here.**

## Monument Time-Line

1832 **July: Cholera outbreak**
**August: Cholera Burial Ground made available.**
**5th November: Epidemic over.**
**1347 cases. 402 dead**

1834 **11th Dec: Cornerstone laid**

1835 **11th April:**
**Last top stone laid**

1839 **January:**
**Damaged in gales**

1883 **Burial ground closed**

1899 **Council leases ground from Duke of Norfolk. Grounds opened**

1900 **By this time walls, railings and access steps gone. Replaced by grass mound and new railings. Buttresses filled in and lower shaft thickened.**

1930 **Given to Sheffield by Duke.**

1940's **Railings taken for war effort?**

1960's **Tower blocks built**

1973 **Monument Grade II listed**

1981 **Norfolk Road designated conservation area**

1990 **25/26th January:**
**Storm damage.**

1994 **Lightning damage**

1997 **Manor & Castle Development Trust created**

1999 **Disconnected parts taken to Sheffield Airport**

2000/01 **Restoration aims finalised, bids for funding**

2002 **Ongoing bids for funding**

The disease was so awful that people wanted to bury the dead as soon as possible to prevent contamination. Some victims were said to have been hurried away before people made sure they were dead. By November the epidemic had ended and 402 people had died. Thousands more were afflicted and survived.

## A monument is decided upon

People who survived decided to build a memorial to those who had died. They chose land the Duke of Norfolk had provided in his park and a monument was built in 1834 over the graves of the 402 people who had lost their lives. The designer was M E Hadfield, a Sheffield man. The £300 cost came from the remains of funds for fighting the epidemic, public donations and a £50 donation from the Duke of Norfolk. The structure was elegant and ambitious, 21.5 m (70ft) high and made of Rivelin gritstone. Four stone steps led up to the main part of the Gothic Revival style tower, a central shaft supported by flying buttresses. The upper part had niches with statues carved by Earp and Hobbs of Manchester. On top was a cross. When the cornerstone was laid, on Thursday December 11th at 2pm, a glass bottle with an inscription was placed in a prepared cavity:

*"The greatest number of new cases, namely 53 and the greatest number of deaths, namely 27, happening on one day, were reported on the 21st August... during the ten days preceding the 7th October, there occurred only 34 new cases and 11 deaths; and from the 8th of the same month to the 10th November following, when the last sufferer was reported to be cured, there were not more than 15 new cases and 9 deaths."* **Extract from the inscription**

Near the memorial is the grave of Master Cutler, John Blake. On it is an inscription telling he was 49 when he caught the 'calamitous infection'. Only six weeks earlier he had laid the foundation stone of the present Cutlers Hall, Sheffield.

Soon the slender tower was a well known landmark, but the design was structurally ahead of its time. Ambition had overtaken know-how and just four years later the top was blown off in a gale.

In 1883 the burial ground was closed to internments.

In July 1899, the Cholera Monument Grounds reopened after improvements, with 320 yards of iron railings and the flying buttresses filled in for added stability. In early pictures, railings are visible. These later disappeared, probably in the war efforts, when metal was collected for weapons. In 1930, on June 21st, the then Duke of Norfolk gave the land containing the monument to the City Council.

The area, including the Shrewsbury Hospital Almshouses opposite the monument park gates on Norfolk Road, was declared a Conservation Area on January 7, 1981. None of the earlier structural improvements of the Monument proved good enough, however, as in gales on January 25 and 26, 1990, the top blew off again. Repairs were not carried out and stonework was put into storage. In 1994 the remaining part was struck by lightning, causing more damage.

The broken stones were removed from the site to various other locations around Sheffield. In 1996, the monument was designated one of Sheffield's leading heritage sites.

## Shrewsbury Hospital Almshouses, Norfolk Road

Opposite the gates of the Cholera Memorial Park are Shrewsbury Hospital Almshouses.

The almshouses were originally founded in the year 1616 by Gilbert, 7th Earl Shrewsbury. They were first opened by the side of the River Sheaf, but due to repeated flooding were relocated here. The present buildings have a central chapel and garden and are private residences.

## The monument today

Today, only the lower part of the once ambitiously soaring structure still stands, waiting to be made whole again. Two gravestones remain, those of the Master Cutler and of a 7 year old, John Simonite.

In 1997 a feasibility study for repairing the site stated, **"the stone is still available, as are the craft skills."** In 1998, a local businessman, Jim Hurley of SIS Interior Solutions Ltd, donated £20,000 and his firm's expertise to rebuild the monument. This lead to "The Friends of the Cholera Monument' being formed. Other businesses and voluntary groups became involved, including the council and Manor & Castle Development Trust. Also involved were local architects Hadfield, Cawkwell and Davison, a firm founded by original designer M E Hadfield. Sheffield Airport were persuaded to store the stonework securely, until the monument is reassembled. It took three years to trace the scattered stonework.

Schemes to make the monument stronger when it is rebuilt include screwing it to the rock below and securing it with a "cunningly designed nut" possibly in the shape of the original cross which is now lost. A metal bar would run from the cross, through the central shaft and secure the monument to the rock below. The monument would also be floodlit at night. More surveys and viability studies are still underway, as well as lottery funding applications. Hopefully these will enable the repair and revitalisation of this piece of Sheffield's historic past and continue to remind us of those who died in the epidemic.

## Spring-Heeled Jack

Forty years after the monument was placed, a strange legend began...

It was in the spring of 1873 that rumours of a ghost at the site spread. The area would already have been seen as an eerie spot, with people remembering all the dead laid there, victims of the epidemic. This no doubt fuelled the rumour. The ghost was said to haunt the area of the cholera grounds and nearby Clay Wood Quarry. The 'Park Ghost' was soon given the nick-name **Spring Heeled Jack**, as it was said to leap about. This name had already been given to a similar apparition seen in 1830 in the Barnes Common area of London. People said they saw the ghost leap over walls 14ft high, or skim over the ground with 'supernatural swiftness'.

It was reported that a vigilante shot the ghost in the ankle, but it bounded away seemingly unharmed. By May of 1873, the ghost had become more frequently spotted and more adventurous, also appearing at Sky Edge, Arbourthorne and Heeley Bank Road. Local historian Henry Tatton later wrote, in 1934:

*"The Park Ghost, alias Spring-Heeled Jack, could spring like a goat, and jump through five-barred gates like a cat. It used to appear at all times of the night, robed in white and suddenly appeared in front of people, mostly courting couples and then disappeared when anyone tried to get a hold of it. It used to come out of the grounds of the Cholera Monument...springing and jumping about the quarry and over walls...all around the district. People were afraid to go out at night and carried sticks to attack it."*

News of the ghost spread. Hundreds came to catch a glimpse. An extra force of policemen was needed to keep people under control. After several narrow escapes, the 'ghost ceased to appear. This could lead to a suspicion that the 'ghost' was really human, with a strange sense of humour, or taking up a dare or bet, scaring locals and couples and seeing how long he could get away with it!

# Wilson's Snuff Mill

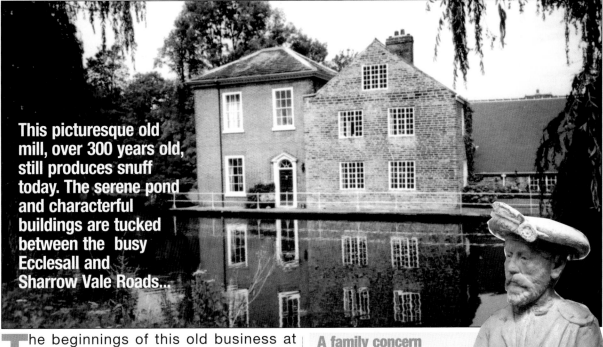

This picturesque old mill, over 300 years old, still produces snuff today. The serene pond and characterful buildings are tucked between the busy Ecclesall and Sharrow Vale Roads...

The beginnings of this old business at Sharrow were in the mid 1700's, when a Mr Thomas Wilson rented the waterwheel and buildings from the Duke of Norfolk. The same overshot waterwheel is still working today, hidden beneath the oldest part of the building.

The building on this site dates from before the snuff mill began in 1737, and was most likely an old farmhouse, with a grinding wheel for trade as was often the case. The place was perhaps expanded to create the mill taken by Thomas.

Wilsons & Co.
SNUFF MANUFACTURERS
SHARROW MILLS
ESTABLISHED 1737

This sign is over the old wooden door into the mills

Next to inherit the mill was Thomas' son Joseph. He was a silversmith and was associated with Boulsover, the inventor of Sheffield Plate. He had various trades, including making scythes and shears, but eventually, sometime in the 1730's, he learned the formula for making snuff and used the old grinding mill for this. By 1750 snuff making was the bulk of his business. These mills at Sharrow are said to be the world's oldest.

In 1746 a fire destroyed some of the mill and stock. There is a fire engine from 1797 still on site and now restored (below).

## A family concern

At first the mill had been called Sharrow Mills, but after Thomas and Joseph there followed another six generations of the Wilson family at the mill and it became known as Wilson's Snuff Mills. Still Wilsons & Company (Sharrow) Ltd today, it is owned and also run by members of the same family that had originally begun the business.

## Modernisation

The waterwheel, using the River Porter for power, was supplemented In the 1790's with steam power. The steam engine was housed at the back of the original building. In the 1900s new mill buildings were added, with a corridor joining them to the original buildings. A tall chimney was also added to the mills, and can be seen on early photographs of the site. This chimney was demolished around the mid 1980s.

The waterwheel was still working however, as it is today, though now it is just run every so often to exercise it and not used for actual production.

Snuff taking became popular in England in the 1700s, but was known in France before that. It was also used earlier in Scotland, due to that country's connections with the French court. Because of this Scottish connection, the image of a Highlander in full kilt was used to advertise the selling of snuff.

## Origins of snuff taking

Snuff is made from finely powdered tobacco leaves. The leaves are matured and dried and then ground and sieved. At Wilson's they were ground in oak mortars by iron pestles.

Natural oils, such as attar of roses and jasmine are added to produce a scent. The powder is then matured in wood.

Snuff is sniffed directly into the nostrils, not reaching the lungs like cigarettes and cigars.

The habit is thought to have started in central and South America, with Spanish invaders bringing the habit back to Europe. Taking it was believed to clear the nose and help prevent colds and catarrh.

## Nose tickling variety

The snuff was packaged in barrels, boxes and bladders. Recipes are still the same.

Flavours include older blends, with recipes being known only by two members of the Wilson family in each generation since 1737, such as Wallflower, Rose of Sharrow, Royal George, Jockey Club, Crumbs of Comfort, Aniseed and Eucalyptus, S.P., S.S., Tom Buck, Sharrow Medicated, Irish High Toast and Queen's Extra Strong, as well as new additions like Super Menthol, SM 500, Rum and Blackberry, Vanilla, Irish Whiskey, Tangerine, Honey Menthol and Prime Minister.

The most commonly taken is perhaps the one called "SP", named after a battle off the coast of a Spanish Port, called Vigo, in 1702. Captured Spanish galleons had a large cargo of snuff, which was taken to London and sold, causing a new fashion of snuff taking in the city. This snuff was called 'Spanish', but this was eventually shortened to SP, resulting in the name.

Two varieties of the snuff on sale today in their metal boxes

The snuffs are divided into four categories: The SP Varieties, Mentholated Snuffs, Scented Snuffs and Fruit, Spice and Flower Flavours.

Still packing the tins of Wilson's snuff by hand in 1967. Now it is an automated task and much less labour intensive

**Above are the old grinding mortars and pestles, covered in a layer of brown tobacco dust. Right is the shaft below that leads up from the waterwheel shaft. This was turned by the waterwheel, and turned the equipment in the grinding room.**

## Snuff boxes

By the eighteenth century snuff-taking was widespread throughout the world. Somewhere to keep the powder was needed and the practical answer of snuff boxes quickly turned into an art form. Many of the boxes were highly decorated, with miniature paintings and intricate enamelwork, jewels and silver.

## Legacy

The Snuff Mill today is partly Grade II listed. The waterwheel still turns now and again, but the modernised business using other power still grinds away, making snuff as it has done for over 300 years. The output has expanded to include cigars and filter tips for today's markets.

The old grinding mortars and pestle are still in place, covered in a brown film of tobacco dust. The cogs and shafts for the old water power are still there too. Old barrels and clay pipes decorate the place, as do many old Scotsman advertising statues.

■ The mill is not open to the public and is private property. However, more details can be found on their website, where snuff can be ordered: **www.snuffs-r-us.com**

Or send enquiries to:

**Wilsons & Co (Sharrow) Ltd, PO Box 32, Sharrow Mills, Sheffield S11 8PL.**

**Tel. +44 (0)114 266 2677**

**Fax. +44 (0)114 267 0504**

**E-mail. Info@snuffs-r-us.com**

**E-mail. Snuff4you@aol.com**

# Anglican Cathedral
### Sheffield

In Sheffield's bustling centre, surrounded by offices, shops, supertram, buses and traffic, is an oasis of calm in the form of the city's Anglican Cathedral...

The Cathedral Church of St. Peter and St. Paul, to give the Cathedral its full name, is one of Sheffield's oldest buildings, a place of worship and community focus for centuries.

## The beginnings

It is thought that the site of the Cathedral has been used for worship since around 800AD. The first church recorded was built here about 1100AD, earlier records could have been destroyed by William The Conqueror. A Saxon cross from the site (now in the British Museum) was found in a cutler's workshop, being used as a trough. It is highly carved and shows knotwork and an archer (shown above right).

A definite record of the Archbishop of York dedicating a church here in 1280 exists. This church was pulled down and rebuilt in 1430. The oldest part of the present Cathedral, the chancel and sanctuary, date from this time. Stones from the earlier church, decorated with a Norman 'dog-tooth' pattern, can still be seen in the east wall. The 1430 church was built in the shape of a cross.

## Inside the Cathedral

### The Shrewsbury Chapel

Later, in 1520, this cruciform shape was changed when The Shrewsbury Chapel (now the Sanctuary of the Lady Chapel) was added. It was used by the Earls of Shrewsbury and contains tombs from the family. The altar top is medieval. The two Shrewsbury tombs are very grand. On the left is the tomb of the Fourth Earl of Shrewsbury in his order of the Garter robes. On either side are his two wives. This tomb dates from 1538. On the right (pictured right, is a monument to the Sixth Earl of Shrewsbury, the one who guarded Mary Queen of Scots, who died in 1590. He was the last husband of Bess of Hardwick. When he died she built Hardwick Hall.

Later, in the year 1777, an extension was built to balance The Shrewsbury Chapel. It was vestries for the clergy to begin with, but later became the Chapel of St. Katherine. Other improvements were carried out at the same time and pews were put in. The church became a Cathedral in 1914 when the Diocese of Sheffield was created out of the Diocese of York.

At the end of World War 1, a grand plan was devised by an architect called Sir Charles Nicholson, which would have changed the shape of the building immensely. Delays and World War II meant that these plans never came to fruition in full.

The Cathedral, in the city centre

When the war was over the plans still were not completed as the cost was considered too great. A less extensive plan was used instead, in 1966, which included extending the nave by 28ft, providing a new chapel of St George and adding a new entrance and lantern.

The Cathedral pulpit

### The St. George's Chapel

This was originally to be the Sanctuary in plans drawn by the architect Nicholson. Now it is St George's chapel dedicated to the military and those who died in war. There are some unusual stained glass windows and also a flag from HMS Sheffield. The chapel railings are made from swords and bayonets.

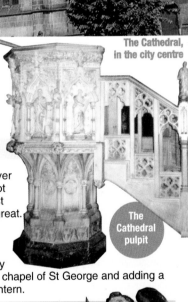
Sixth Earl of Shrewsbury's Tomb.

This rosy cheeked statue holds a shield with a St George cross, but is St. Michael (because of the wings) not St George.

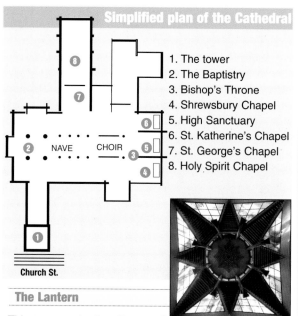

## Simplified plan of the Cathedral

1. The tower
2. The Baptistry
3. Bishop's Throne
4. Shrewsbury Chapel
5. High Sanctuary
6. St. Katherine's Chapel
7. St. George's Chapel
8. Holy Spirit Chapel

Angels and an Agnus Dei on a screen in the Cathedral

### Some interesting carvings

### The Lantern

This represents the Crown of Thorns. The original 1966 lantern was replaced in 1998 by a new one, with glass by artist Amber Hiscott. The windows symbolise how the Holy Spirit (gold and reds) turn conflict (blues and violets) into healing and harmony (greens).

### The Chapel of the Holy Spirit

This is beyond the St George's Chapel. There is a fine glass window by Christopher Webb (1940). There are other windows by him in the St Katherine's Chapel (east window) and some in the Chapter House (not open to the public).

### The High Sanctuary

The focus of the Cathedral. The central bust on the left wall is the earliest known work of sculptor Sir Francis Chantrey (1805).

### The Chancel

The chancel contains the Bishop's throne or *cathedra*. This is where the word cathedral comes from. There are also wonderful carved golden angels along the roofline.

Right: The possible sheela-na-gig

These carvings are found in the Shrewsbury Chapel. The *green man* (above), is an ancient symbol of rebirth and is on the central roof beam as you look back to the entrance. He has two crossed swords above him, a possible connection to old pagan beheading rituals such as in the old tale Gawain and the Green Knight. There are more green men scattered in the Cathedral decorations, on roof bosses and above the altar window. Opposite him is what appears to be a *sheela na gig*, an ancient fertility symbol of life. Above this is an Agnes Dei, or Lamb of God, carrying a flag with a cross. This is a Christian symbol of sacrifice and resurrection.

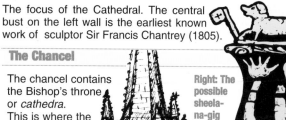

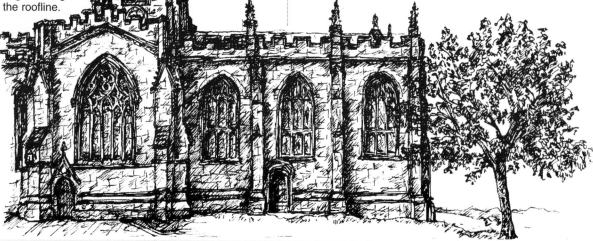

■ Sheffield Cathedral: Telephone (0114) 2753434   ■ website: www.sheffield-cathedral.org.uk   ■ e mail: enquiries@sheffield-cathedral.org.uk

# Around the Cathedral

## Boys' Charity School

At the bottom of East Parade on the right of the Cathedral is a building which used to be a Boys' School.

The original building was erected in 1710 and rebuilt in 1825 (present building). It held 100 boys. The school was moved to Psalter Lane in 1911.

If you look up to the roof of the building from near York Street you can see railings along the edge. These were added so that the boys could play safely on the roof. This was needed because there were complaints from the church, (now the cathedral), when the boys played in the churchyard.

## Girls Charity School

At the other side of the Cathedral, on St James' Row, there was a girls' school. The building is still there (see right) and bears a semi circular plaque near the roof with the words

**"This Charity School for poor girls was built by public subscription AD 1786".**

## The 'Priory'

This chapel like building, on a street at the left of the Cathedral, is now a pub called The Priory. It was not actually a priory before this, but a building used by the church to give evening classes, as the Pawson and Brailsford Guide (1879) mentions:

*"CHURCH OF ENGLAND EDUCATIONAL INSTITUTE- ...was set on foot in 1840, but was carried on with comparatively little success until 1856, when it took a new start under the auspices of the Rev James Moorhouse, who came forward to assist the unpaid teachers who had borne the burden for so many years. This handsome building in St James' Street was opened in 1860, having being erected by public subscription."*

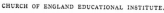
CHURCH OF ENGLAND EDUCATIONAL INSTITUTE.

## Old Synagogue

On North Church Street, at the back of the Cathedral off Campo Lane, is a Grade II listed building, an old synagogue, with Hebrew lettering around the entrance.

At the time of writing, the cathedral is raising money to build a new Community Resources Centre, with purpose built access from Campo Lane. It will include a training room, IT facilities, the Breakfast Project and Archer Cafe. The campaign to raise the £6.5m needed began May 2000.

### CATHEDRAL SERVICE TIMES

**Sunday**
8am Holy Communion
10am Morning prayer
10.30am Sung Eucharist
18.30pm Evensong
**Mon -Fri**
7.30am Morning Prayer
8am Eucharist
12noon Peace prayers
15.30pm Evening Prayers
17.45 Evensong
**Saturday**
10am Morning prayer
10.30 Eucharist
12 Peace prayers
15.00pm Evensong

This strange turban-clad Head is found on Talbot Chambers, North Church Street

31

## Paradise Square

At the back of the Cathedral is an area called Paradise Square, a time capsule of fine Georgian buildings around a cobbled centre.

Before the square existed, the area from Campo Lane to West Bar was a large Orchard. Campo Lane is said to derive from the latin word Campus, referring to the old grounds around the Cathedral.

Development of the area began around 1739, with many fine houses being built in this rural setting. The Georgian middle classes coveted town houses there, which were built in the neo-classical style, with pillars and fine stucco (hard plaster) decoration.

Solicitors, doctors and other professionals moved in to the sought after square. One of these was a Dr Daniel Davies, who later moved to London and attended at the birth of Queen Victoria, as well as translating a work about insanity.

Another famous resident of the Square was local sculptor Francis Chantrey, from Norton. He had lodgings at No 24 when he finished his apprenticeship. Whilst living there he advertised in the local newspaper, then *The Iris*, asking for clients for portraits. He lived there until 1802, before moving to London.

In 1771 a wealthy man called Thomas Broadbent opened The Sheffield Bank nearby at Hartshead House (still there on the corner of Campo Lane and St Peter's Close). It didn't go too well, for in 1782, the bank crashed with debts and Broadbent lost his property and wealth, including the bank.

A bricked up door in the archway on the left of Hartshead House was probably blocked around this time.

John Wesley, founder of Methodism, preached in the square. In 1779 he drew a crowd which he said was "the largest congregation I ever saw on a weekday." A plaque commemorating his visits here was unveiled in 1951.

An ornate balcony to be seen in the square

mostly pottery. Paradise Square gained the nickname of "Pot Square".

No 1 Paradise Square used to be "The House of Help for Friendless Girls and Young Women." This opened in 1880, taking in the homeless and training them for domestic service if they wished to find employment.

In 1908 the home moved to larger premises at No.17, and had 26 beds. During World War 1, many women visiting injured husbands in Sheffield made use of the facility. The home remained until 1940, when it was destroyed in the Sheffield Blitz on December 12.

Also in the square, at the building with the most ornate balcony, No.18 shown above, was Hebblethwaite's Academy. This fancy residence was originally a Freemason's Lodge, but changed to the academy in 1811, when Edward Hebblethwaite opened his school. He had seen the premises for rent and saw the potential for a fee paying school for the middle classes. The school was there until 1937, but Hebblethwaite himself retired in 1865. There were once steps leading up to the balcony, from which many heartfelt speeches have issued forth.

Some of the old buildings

A market used to be held in the Square every October This was a hiring fair, where the country people came into town to find work. In the year 1796, a man even sold his wife there for just sixpence.

**The old rainwater header**

By 1808 the market had changed to that of one that sold

Chartists also used Paradise Square, with meetings there in the early 19th Century. The group were called Chartists as they followed a six point charter, which included calling for work for all men over 21, and the right to secret ballots. In September 1838, there was a procession from Barkers Pool to the Square, a gathering of thousands from all over the county. Some of the meetings became violent and so further ones were banned. One meeting, in August 1839, led to 70 arrests and in September of the same year, a riot caused the Dragoons to be called out, with 36 arrests following. But the Chartists still met illegally, often by torchlight on Sky Edge, until the momentum of the movement died out in the 1840's.

There are many interesting features to spot in the Square, including a lead rainwater header, dated 1777, some fine streetlamps and of course lots of old cobbles .

**A plaque to the doctor who helped at Queen Victoria's birth. He once lived here.**

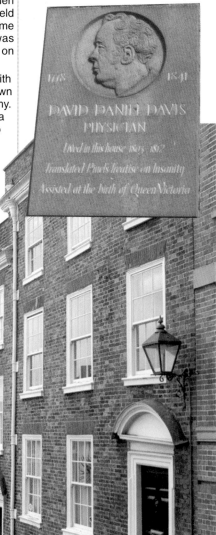

# Revolution House

**Revolution House,
High Street,
Old Whittington S41 9LA
Te: Chesterfield Museums
on (01246) 345727
Open April to September,
10am to 4pm**

*An old ale house near Chesterfield was the plotting place for an act of treason to overthrow a King...*

In the late 17th century, in Old Whittington, three miles north of Chesterfield, was a pub called the Cock and Pynot (a dialect word for magpie). It is now called the Revolution House, a reminder of its history.

## The old house

James ll, who had succeeded his brother Charles as King in 1685, was fated only to reign for three years. He was a Catholic convert, which upset many of his protestant subjects. Catholics were fined or imprisoned at the time for practising their faith. Some people wanted to get rid of James, for a protestant monarch. James had an ally in the King of France, Louis XIV, though many others were against him

William Cavendish, the Earl of Devonshire, was one who plotted to overthrow James. It was in the Cock and Pynot that Cavendish, along with Thomas Osbourne, Earl of Danby and a Mr John D'Arcy, met and arranged their part in assisting William of Orange's plan to land in Britain and take the throne.

The Cock and Pynot, with thatched roof and attractively wobbly appearance, was a farmhouse before it became an ale house. Remnants of the old lifestyle then include a salt cupboard on the right of the fireplace. Salt was very expensive at the time, and this cupboard would have kept it dry. It would be kept locked to protect the salt from theft. Animals would have been kept in the room on the right of the house. A 'squeeze door' small enough to keep the animals from wandering into the other room was used. It was the practice at the time for many farm houses to brew their own ale. The ale here must have been good enough to attract lots of customers and so it became known as an alehouse. The animal's room was replaced by a parlour.

## Plotting in the pub

In 1688, the three men mentioned, opposed to James' plans for the country, met under cover of a hunting trip, to discuss how they would support the attempt by William of Orange (a Protestant) and his wife Mary (James' daughter) to take the throne. Mary was regarded as James' legitimate heir by the rebels.

The weather turned bad and so the men went to The Cock and Pynot, to carry on the meeting. They sat in the parlour of the alehouse and talked of their plans to raise the North and Midlands to support William. The Earl of Devonshire later marched on Derby with 500 men, carrying the banner of William of Orange. From Derby they marched to Nottingham, where they met with Danby, who had marched from York. This was timed to coincide with William of Orange's landing at Torbay, Devon, with 13,000 or so men, on November 5, 1688.

At Salisbury he was met by James and his army. James and his army were defeated. James had already fled to London, then tried to reach France but was caught. He was brought back to London, but no agreement with William could be reached, and James left secretly for France. He died, still deposed, in St Germain in 1701.

William of Orange and his wife Mary were crowned at Westminster Abbey on 11 April 1689. Thus the revolution was a success.

## Marking the events

On November 5, 1788, a hundred years on, a celebration of the events was held at the old Cock and Pynot, still used as a pub but nicknamed the Revolution House because of the plottings.

The man responsible for organising celebrations was Samuel Pegge, the Rector of Whittington from 1751-1796. Pegge wrote an account of the event:

*"There were no less than fifty coaches and chaises with horses dressed with orange ribbons...there were about 1000 on foot.. and about 300 on horseback..At half past six the fireworks, by an Italian artist began."*

By 1789 a new building had been erected behind the old pub. This is the present Cock and Magpie, built by landlord George Glossop. The original pub was let out to tenants. Thomas Cartwright was the first recorded tenant.

**Chesterfield's Coat of arms bears a Cock and Pynot. The motto 'Aspire' is a pun (a spire)**

By 1888, The Revolution House had fallen partly into ruin and events were a little forgotten. An advert was put into the Derbyshire Times in October to raise interest. It worked and a large crowd attended. A 1788 banner was displayed and there was a procession and speeches, a banquet and fireworks.

## A new lease of life

The old inn was used by tenants, until 1937, when it was taken over by Chesterfield Corporation. It was restored and reopened as a museum on October 28th, 1938, by the 10th Duke of Devonshire. The Revolution House is now cared for by Chesterfield Borough Council. It was refurbished in 1988 when a new audio visual room was added. Also in the museum, is the 'plotting chair.' It is a replica of a chair said to have been used by the Earl of Devonshire at their meeting. The original chair is at Hardwick Hall. There is a display about the house and the revolution, as well as an informative video. Admission is free.

# The Crooked Spire

**The market town of Chesterfield is a lively and pretty place to visit. Towering over the streets full of history towers its most famous landmark, the crooked spire...**

## Church plan key
1. Main entrance
2. Church shop
3. Nave
4. North aisle
5. South aisle
6. St. Peter's Chapel
7. St Oswald's Chapel
8. Lesser Lady Chapel
9. Lady Chapel
10. Foljambe tombs
11. St Catherine's Chapel
12. Holy Cross Chapel

The famous twisted spire of St Mary and All Saints church, Chesterfield

Even if Chesterfield's famous church did not owe it's celebrity status to a twisted spire, the lovely old building would still have plenty to recommend it.

### Chesterfield's origins

Chesterfield is an old market town. Earlier still it was a frontier of two British tribes, the Coritani and the Brigantes, but later became a Roman settlement, offering a good vantage point to keep an eye on the Britons. By 140 AD the Romans had gone. The place was later called Chesterfield by the Anglo Saxons.

Chesterfield's famous landmark is on the Parish Church of St Mary and All Saints. The quirky looking spire of this lovely church has become a symbol of the town itself, an instantly recognisable accident of architecture.

There were earlier churches on the site, but work on the present church began in the thirteenth century and lasted for almost 200 years. Guide books say it was formally dedicated in 1234, but this is now disputed by some, who say it was a mistake caused by misreading a document. The church was not fully finished until around 1400, with the spire as the last phase.

Many people would have passed a lifetime watching the building progress and never seeing the result. Most of the nave and tower of the present church date from the early 14th century. It is a very large church and served many of the surrounding villages, such as Newbold and Whittington, which are now part of the borough of Chesterfield.

### That famous spire

The wooden, lead coated spire was the final finishing touch. It was of course straight then, towering 228ft (70m) over the Derbyshire landscape. Now it is warped and twisted, making it an outstanding and unusual landmark. It doesn't seem to have anything attaching it to the tower, except for its own weight! A pointer on the floor inside the church, beneath the tower, shows where the point of the spire is now and how far from the original centre point of the tower it has moved

There are many legends and theories as to how the spire became crooked...

A rather rude version is that a true virgin once was wed at the church and the spire was so surprised that it bent down to get a better look! The more polite version is that she was so beautiful that the spire wanted to get closer to admire her...

Another tale is that the devil alighted on the spire for a rest and church incense went up his nose and made him sneeze, twisting the spire with the effort.

A popular theory is that unseasoned wood was used and as it dried out it twisted out of shape, with the weight of the lead adding to the problem. Green or unseasoned wood was normally used for buildings at the time, however, as it was easier to work.

**Simplified plan of church interior**

Tradition has it that the problem could have been due to builders becoming scarce in the late 1300's, because of the Black Death, a plague caused by the fleas from black rats. This is probably unlikely. Big projects were still rare and people were still learning and developing the methods.

Access to the tower is up 144 steps and there are frequent tours up there.

**THE BELLS** There are ten bells, dating from 1820. Before that there was a set of eight bells, and also a smaller bell called a shriving bell, or the curfew bell. It was rung at nightfall to summon French prisoners of war, once kept in Chesterfield between 1804 and 1814, to their quarters

In the porch as you enter the church the floor is lined with old gravestones, including one to 'Thomas Smith, musician of this town' - who died in 1785 aged 68.

# Inside the church of St Mary and All Saints

## The High Altar

This is the focal point of the church. The lamp in front of it is probably a copy of one from Venice. It has a red light which is left burning constantly to symbolise the presence of God.

The elaborate panel at the back of the altar (called a reredos) was made in 1898 and has the Virgin Mary and child as the centre image. It was plain wood until 1936, when it was coloured.

The reredos

## The Lady Chapel

This is often referred to as the Foljambe chapel, as in here are some of the most impressive monuments in the church. They are for the Foljambe family, Sherriffs of the County of Derby and ironically later members of the same Catholic family that were later implicated in murders at the church in 1422.

They lived at Walton Hall in Chesterfield. The name means 'Foolish or (strange) Leg' and a carving of a single leg, severed at the thigh, (the family symbol), can be found perched on the tomb on the right hand wall. The family motto was 'Stand Firm', very hard with only one leg! A little subtle humour coming to us down the ages perhaps?

The tombs are made from alabaster and were made during the years 1510-1604. The earliest tomb is on the left and is of Henry Foljambe and his wife Benedicta. A kneeling figure is thought to be the thirteen year old Sir Thomas. It seems to have been broken at some time and given a rather too large head from another statue. The centre tomb is of Sir Godfrey (died 1585) and his wife. The tomb on the right is of another Godfrey (died 1594) and his wife. The wall part of this tomb has the date 1592 so it was made before his death. At the side of this tomb leans a huge whale bone, almost now the same colour as the darkened alabaster. No one knows why or when it was placed there, though it was mentioned in a local newspaper in 1837. There is also a huge, elaborate candalabrum, one of a pair of candalabra, hanging from the ceiling. A gift to the church in 1760, it holds 48 candles. The other one is in St Catherine's Chapel

The large clock near the Lady Chapel is around 200 years old and was given as a gift to the church in 1995, in the memory of three sisters of the Orwin family. The oak case, now dark with age has attractive carvings, including one of a crucifixion scene.

Right: One of the ornate Foljambe tombs in the church

## The Lesser Lady Chapel

This is another, smaller Lady Chapel. There is usually only one in a church so this is very unusual. In here is a 14th century piscina. This is where the chalice used for the mass was washed. There is a copy of the painter Bellini's Madonna and child.

## St Catherines's Chapel

This is the farthest left from the High Altar. It is named after St Catherine of Alexandria, who was tortured for her Christian faith by being tied to a flaming spiked wheel. She gave her name to the firework the Catherine Wheel. There is a 14th century piscina in this chapel too. On the wall opposite the altar is a lovely winged cherub, a monument to a Hannah Stanforth, who died in 1771 and two of her grandchildren who died as infants.

## Holy Cross Chapel

In this chapel, in a glass case, is kept a lovely medieval processional cross, known as the Hunloke cross after the family which gave it to the church. It was restored in 1996.

## The Rood Beam

Rood is an old word for cross and the rood beam was where the cross was positioned, high up, usually across an arch in front of the altar. The one in this church is quite a modern one, dating from 1915. It was later painted and gilded. The cross, with Christ, has Mary on the left and St John on the right. The figures were carved by a Belgian refugee.

## The Font

The font, for baptism, is probably the oldest item in the church. It dates from around 890-1050. It has leaves and a cross carved on it, though it is very worn and hard to make out. It was removed from the church at some time and was found buried in the vicarage garden in 1898. It was placed in its present position in 1953.

The font

The panel at the back of the Foljambe tombs is full of wonderful carvings. At the top right is a rather overgrown cherub, representing youth, with some kind of rattle or windmill affair in his hand. At the left is old age and in the centre a skeletal figure representing death. In his left hand he has an arrow and in his right a shovel, ready to bury people. In the panel below that a shrouded corpse lays on a trestle table. Below that are carvings to do with death- a shovel, bones, a skull, and a winged hourglass.

## The Screen

On the wooden screen near the altar are carvings of kings on the throne at the time of important events in the life of the church. These kings are Edward the Confessor, Henry lll, Richard ll and George VI.

The effigy to the right of St. Peters's altar in the south nave aisle is that of a priest in 14th century dress. A lion lies at his feet.

## The Lectern

This is where readings from the bible take place Lecterns are often in the form of an Eagle. This one dates from 1890. The eagle is also a symbol of the apostle St John.

### Pulpit
This elaborately carved place to read the sermon from is Jacobean, made around 1620

The lectern, with eagle decoration

The pulpit

## Murder in the Church

In 1266, St Mary's and All Saints saw some gruesome events. Some of the Barons in the land rebelled against the King, Henry lll, resulting in the so named 'Battle of Chesterfield'. The leader of the Barons was a man called Robert Ferrers, the Earl of Derby. The King sent an army to Chesterfield to put an end to the rebellion, and Ferrers lost. Some say the battle took place by the church but no one knows for sure. Ferrers was said to have been found hiding under wool bags in the church. He was arrested and later imprisoned at Windsor.

Other violent goings on were on January 1, 1422, when an armed Lancastrian force of 200, led by local landowners Thomas and Richard Foljambe, attacked the church during a mass.

## Stained Glass

There are many fine examples of stained glass work, some by artist Christopher Webb. The most impressive is probably the West Window or Judgement window, and shows scenes from the life of Joshua.

A new Anniversary Window, to commemorate the 750th anniversary of the church, was added in 1984 and shows Chesterfield through the ages.

At the right hand side of the Lady Chapel is this lovely set of leaded windows. The scene is a man holding a child's hand. The dedication is to a John Henry Walker, who died February 4, 1844, aged just 16 years.

This statue, shown right, stands in a very ornate gold niche and can be found near St Peter's chapel.

### Church service times

| Sunday | Other masses |
|---|---|
| **8am Mass, 10.30am** Sung mass **6.30pm** evensong | **Mon:** 12.15am **Tues:** 9.30am **Wed:** 9.30am **Thu:** 5.30pm **Fri:** 12.15 **Sat:** 9.30 |
| Mon-Sat **9am** Matins **5pm** Evensong | |

**Telephone no: 01246 206 506**

## French Prisoners

During the Napoleonic wars, French prisoners of war were kept at Chesterfield. They were mostly officers. Some were employed making gloves.

They were allowed a daily walk, but had to return by 8pm. The earlier mentioned Curfew Bell was their call back to their quarters .

One of these French prisoners is buried in the churchyard. His tomb is in the part of the graveyard nearest the Rutland public house, near the wall along the side of the church. It reads:

*En Memoire de Francois Raingeard age de 30 ans le 10 Mars 1812*
(In memory of Francois Raingeard age 30 years the 10 March 1812)

*Stop traveller! If in life's journey sympathy has found a seat in thy breast Thou'lt drop a pitying tear to the memory of one who fell a sacrifice in friendship's pious cause.*

*Requiescat in pace*
(rest in peace)

The translation above is from a display in the Chesterfield Museum, which is a short distance from the church.

Peeks at the Past

## The windlass

A large wooden wheel, called a windlass or builders' wheel, was used to turn ropes and operate pulleys to lift the building materials for churches.

The load was attached to a rope that was wound around the axle of the wheel. Men then stepped inside the wheel itself and treaded it round, rather like oversized hamsters, which raised the load.

The wheel used to build Chesterfield Parish Church still survives, and can be seen in the museum near the church. It was discovered in the church tower in 1947 and restored in 1994. It is 15 feet (4,6m) in diameter.

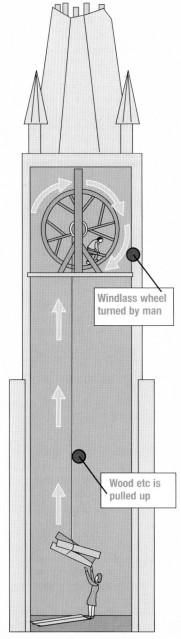

Windlass wheel turned by man

Wood etc is pulled up

Diagram based on a model at Chesterfield Museum

## Around the town

### THE SHAMBLES

This area is named after the word 'Fleshambles' and was where animals were slaughtered and the butchers' shops were found.

Also here can be seen a lovely old building, The Royal Oak pub, which dates fron the 16th century.

### THE FALCON INN

This half timbered building, dating from around 1600, is on the corner of South Street and the Low Pavement was probably built as a house, later turned into The Falcon Inn. It has imposing pillars at its entrance.

### SPITAL

This area takes its name from a now long gone leper hospital that stood at the foot of Hady Hill.

### PEACOCK Heritage Centre

Apart from the church, this is Chesterfield's oldest surviving building. It dates from around 1500 and was built as a house, and used later as a meeting hall.

**Chesterfield Tourist Information Centre has many useful leaflets and books about Chesterfield. Telephone no: 01246 345777**

### KNIFESMITHSGATE

This is a street where buildings have been decorated in a mock Tudor style in the building development of the 1920's and 1930's.

The word 'gate' is a Danish word for street, dating back to the times when Danes were in control in the area.

Knifesmithgate is named after a family of that name.

**Left is one of the faces carved on the mock tudor frontage of Knifesmithsgate**

The Royal Oak public house, which dates to the 16th century

## GEORGE STEPHENSON

This well known Victorian engineer has links with Chesterfield.

He was the chief engineer of the North Midland Railway, linking Leeds and Derby and moved to Chesterfield when the railway reached there in 1840. He lived at Tapton House, on the outskirts of the town.

He died at Tapton House in August 1848 and is buried at Holy Trinity Church on Newbold Road.

He was a friend of the head gardener at Chatsworth, Sir Joseph Paxton. (Paxton was the builder of the Crystal Palace in London).

Stephenson shared Paxton's passion for gardening and one of his projects was to grow straight cucumbers with the aid of a glass cylinder, which is still at the Chesterfield Museum.

He was later remembered with the building of the Stephenson Memorial Hall, on Corporation Street, which now houses the Town Museum and the Pomegranate Theatre.

■ **Chesterfield Museum is at St Mary's Gate, close to the Crooked Spire Parish Church. Open 10 - 4pm except Wednesday and Sunday. Telephone : (01246) 345727 Admission free.**

# The Eyre Chapel

## This little gem can be found in a field tucked behind the old Nag's Head pub on Newbold Road in Chesterfield...

This old and tiny chapel is at the highest point of Newbold village. It dates from the mid 1200's, when the Normans arrived in the area and is dedicated to St Martin.

The chapel gets its name from the later owners the Eyre family. The original roof would probably have been made of thatch. This stone rectangular building has pinnacles on the four corners, with a larger pinnacle on the west gable. There is a lovely view to the rear. At the side of the chapel is a cross commemorating members of the Eyre family: Vincent Thomas Eyre, Arthur Henry Eyre and Ferdinand John Eyre 1887

There are no openings on its north side, but on the south side there are two doors. The smaller door, known as the priest's door, has a Norman tympanum (a semi circular panel) above the door, which is very worn so the details of the carving on it cannot be seen. This is thought to be older than the present building, being 11th century, so must have come from an earlier structure. There are two windows, which have two glass sections, or lights, in each of them. The larger door was added in alterations between 1475 and 1525, and the side windows were enlarged form the original Norman ones.

Inside, there is a stone altar at the east end of the building. There are some lovely wooden beams in the ceiling, three of which have 15th century carved roof bosses.

There are also two modern stained glass windows. The one on the left commemorates the Eyre family and the right window is in memory of a man called Graham Robinson, who led the fight to keep the historic market place of Chesterfield, shown in the glass, from destruction. There are also two well dressing style coats of arms hung on the wall.

**The Nags Head pub is on (01246) 230682**

Lining the walls are shields bearing memorials and the motto 'Neminem Metui Innocens'. (An innocent man fears no one). The roof is beamed and the walls whitewashed stone.

In the early 16th century, the practising of the Roman Catholic faith became outlawed by the King, Henry VIII. The Eyre family, a noble family of the Peak District, was catholic and members of the family were hidden by shepherds in various places rather than give up their faith. (A shepherd can be seen in the window commemorating the Eyre family, to acknowledge this). The family owned Newbold and had to sell it, but kept the chapel, the yard near it and the Nags Head public House.

By 1685, King James II was on the throne, so it became possible for Catholics to worship again and the chapel was again in use. When William of Orange took the throne in 1689, protestants attacked and looted the Eyre Chapel Gravestones and monuments were smashed or taken away.

The chapel was left to become derelict, being used as a place to keep cows.

Later, new acts of Parliament, in 1791 and 1829, enabled Catholics to practice their faith. Members of the Eyre family then renovated the chapel and used it as a mortuary chapel of rest.

The landlord and landlady of the Nag's Head kept the keys and cleaned and swept it. This is still the case.

The large stone cross is a memorial to further restoration of the chapel in 1887 and to the reinterment of 12 members of the Eyre family in the crypt beneath the stone floor. 1926 was the date of the last burial here.

In 1949, a member of the Eyre family, Capt. R F Eyre-Huddlestone, gave the chapel to the church diocese of the area. At this time Newbold was growing apace and up to four masses a day were said at the chapel.

A new, larger church was built in 1965, a short distance away at Littlemoor. This meant that the Eyre Chapel was unused once more. It was used as a store and workshop and fell into ruin again.

In the early 1980's, moves were made by the Chesterfield Civic Society to save the building. This resulted in a newly restored building, opened on 26th September 1987 by the Duchess of Devonshire. Now it is used as a village hall, though Roman Catholic masses are still celebrated there several times a year.

The Eyre Chapel is available for hire.
Bookings: Mrs Pam Boult  01246 237622.

# General Cemetery

On Cemetery Road is an enclave full of lovely examples of the stonemason's art, left in memory of those departed, who now share their rest with birds and flowers

This wonderful old graveyard has no less than nine listed buildings and monuments within its atmospheric walls. These walls would have being placed to keep out the threat of body snatchers, a great possibility at the time when anatomy students were not allowed bodies legally. Around 87,000 people are buried here.

## Beginnings

During the 19th century, births and deaths were rapidly increasing and the churchyards were filling up, so another idea was needed - specially designed places for lots of graves and not always in a churchyard. Private cemeteries were being designated around the country for this task.

The cemetery in Sheffield was decided upon at a meeting at the Cutlers' Hall in 1834. Land was bought from Henry Wilson of Wilsons Snuff Mills, Sharrow. An architect called Samuel Worth won the competition to design the layout and the first burial took place in May 1836.

The entrances are grand. From Cemetery Avenue you pass over a small bridge over the River Porter, through the lion gate, so called because of a lion head carving on the arch. Here small rooms were built, one for the sexton and one for the gravedigger.

Entering the cemetery, to the left along a side path are walled up catacombs. These were not popular and remained unused. Further up the main path on the right is seen the large Non Conformist chapel, also designed by Worth as a centrepiece of his layout, with its greek style appearance and pillars. A dove is carved above the entrance. It is now sadly bricked up and the chapel is unused.

From the Cemetery Road entrance the gate is an Egyptian style portal, bearing a winged sphere. This symbolises the soul or spirit taking flight. The gates bear serpents eating their tails, an old archetypal symbol of eternity or rebirth.

**Non Conformist Chapel and dove**

In 1864 over 70 victims of th Sheffield Flood were brought to this cemetery for burial. Also buried here is John Gunston, who was deputy engineer working on the Dale Dyke dam that burst to cause the flood. He was at first held responsible for the tragedy but later the blame was lifted.

A second phase of the cemetery, for Church of England burials was built in 1850, designed by Robert Marnock who also designed the Botanical Gardens. The large, spired Anglican Chapel is part of this design.

## Decline

By the 1950's the cemetery was very run down and neglected. It was overgrown and many of the monuments were falling into ruin. In 1963 a housing company wanted to buy the land but people opposed this and it didn't happen. In 1980 the council cleared the lower, Anglican part of the cemetery to provide a public green space. Sadly many headstones were crushed as land filler or buried on site before a halt was called.

**Winged sphere from over the gate**

These obelisks used to stand at the entrance on Cemetery Avenue

A serpent eating its tail, from the Egyptian gate.

This is an old image, based on the worm Ouroborous, a symbol of eternity, rebirth or life and death

## Map of the Cemetery showing grave sites

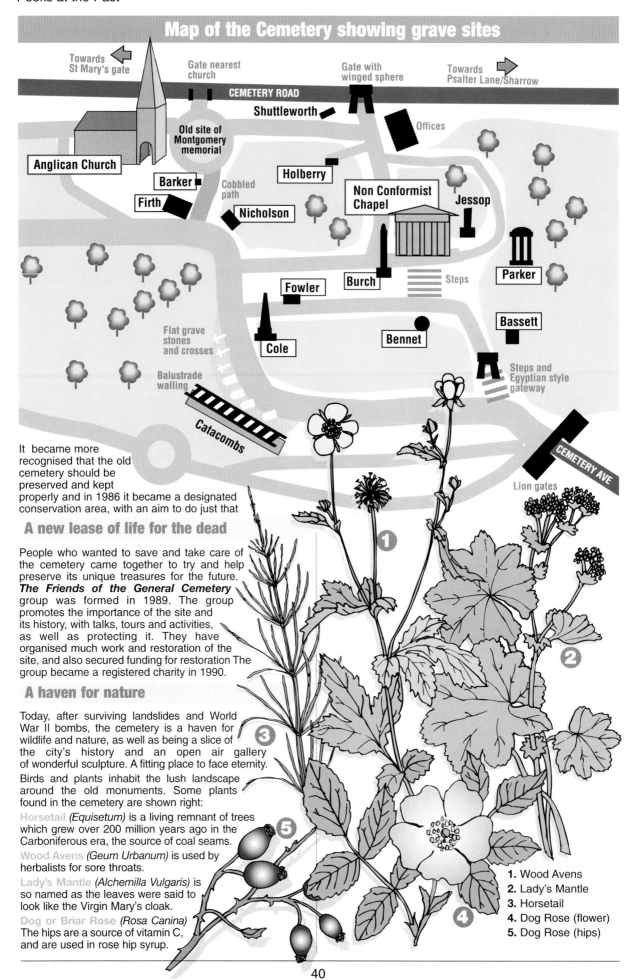

Towards St Mary's gate

Gate nearest church

Gate with winged sphere

Towards Psalter Lane/Sharrow

CEMETERY ROAD

Shuttleworth

Offices

Old site of Montgomery memorial

**Anglican Church**

**Barker**

Cobbled path

**Holberry**

**Non Conformist Chapel**

**Jessop**

**Firth**

**Nicholson**

**Burch**

Steps

**Parker**

**Fowler**

Flat grave stones and crosses

**Cole**

**Bennet**

**Bassett**

Balustrade walling

Steps and Egyptian style gateway

Catacombs

CEMETERY AVE

Lion gates

It became more recognised that the old cemetery should be preserved and kept properly and in 1986 it became a designated conservation area, with an aim to do just that

## A new lease of life for the dead

People who wanted to save and take care of the cemetery came together to try and help preserve its unique treasures for the future. **The Friends of the General Cemetery** group was formed in 1989. The group promotes the importance of the site and its history, with talks, tours and activities, as well as protecting it. They have organised much work and restoration of the site, and also secured funding for restoration The group became a registered charity in 1990.

## A haven for nature

Today, after surviving landslides and World War II bombs, the cemetery is a haven for wildlife and nature, as well as being a slice of the city's history and an open air gallery of wonderful sculpture. A fitting place to face eternity.

Birds and plants inhabit the lush landscape around the old monuments. Some plants found in the cemetery are shown right:

Horsetail *(Equisetum)* is a living remnant of trees which grew over 200 million years ago in the Carboniferous era, the source of coal seams.

Wood Avens *(Geum Urbanum)* is used by herbalists for sore throats.

Lady's Mantle *(Alchemilla Vulgaris)* is so named as the leaves were said to look like the Virgin Mary's cloak.

Dog or Briar Rose *(Rosa Canina)* The hips are a source of vitamin C, and are used in rose hip syrup.

1. Wood Avens
2. Lady's Mantle
3. Horsetail
4. Dog Rose (flower)
5. Dog Rose (hips)

## Some residents

### George Bennet

This Grade II listed monument is for a missionary. It shows Bennet leaning on a globe, with palm trees behind. These represent his well travelled missionary life. He also campaigned against the slave trade. It was erected in 1850, but is now damaged. The drawing shows how it looked.

### George Bassett

Yes, the Liquorice type Bassett. He died in 1886. He had lots of sweet shops in Sheffield, the first one being in 1840, though the famous Allsorts were invented after his death. His gravestone is a rectangular block bearing a shield. It is found just to the right up steps through a small Egyptian styled gateway, on the right of the path up from the lion gate.

### The Cole Brothers

On the right of the main path up from the lion gate, near the stones and crosses laid flat by balustrade fencing, is an obelisk memorial. This is to three brothers of the Cole family, after whom the store in Barkers Pool in Sheffield was named. Their first store was opened in Fargate, at the High Street junction with Church Street, in 1847. The place is still known as Coles Corner by many locals. Now a bank, it has a plaque on the wall to mark the old name. Later the family sold the business to John Lewis Partnership. It moved to the present Barkers Pool location, on the site of the old Albert Hall, in 1963.

### Ralph Barker

Half way up on the left of a smaller cobbled path, near the Anglican Church, can be seen a monument to a Mr Ralph Barker. He was kind enough to help many women who found themselves in difficulty. On his tomb it states he left money to the Deakin Institute, to help the "aged, destitute and unmarried females".

The Anglican Church, derelict and awaiting a new fate

### William Parker

One of the larger monuments is to cutlery exporter William Parker. An elaborate, classical design, it was erected in 1837. Now it is Grade II listed. Around the top are the words 'Blessed are they who die in the Lord." An inscription, relating to his merchant style life, says:

*"To kindred friends and townsmen dear, A Christian merchant slumbers here, Who found while goodly pearls he sought. One pearl of price surpassing thought. Reader do likewise, he who finds and buys that pearl, though he sell all he hath is wise".*

### James Nicholson

This lovely memorial of a woman in prayer dates from 1872 and is Grade II listed. It used to have an angel at each corner, now flown. The Nicholson family were steel industrialists. James commissioned this for his wife Harriet. He and his children now lie here too.

### Thomas Burch

At the front of the Nonconformist Chapel and just to the right is a 15ft column, topped with a veiled urn, a common death symbol. This is for a man called Thomas Burch, alderman in Sheffield for almost twenty years. It was erected by his widow.

Below: The run down interior of the Anglican Church lets in the sunbeams

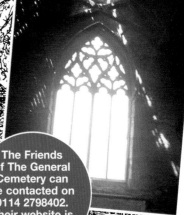

The Friends of The General Cemetery can be contacted on 0114 2798402. Their website is www.fogc.org

## Samuel Holberry (1814-1842)

One of the most historically important graves in the cemetery is that of Samuel Holberry, a hero and figurehead of the Chartist movement in Sheffield.

He was born in Gamston, near Retford in Nottinghamshire, the youngest of nine children, on November 18th 1814. It was a poor family, with his father working as an agricultural labourer. They had a hard time, and the children had hardly any education. Samuel wanted to try and escape this lean and draining existence and at 17 he joined the army.

To try and make up for his lack of education, he went to night school, in Northampton, changing his mind about the army and borrowing money to buy his discharge after three years. He came to Sheffield and worked as a cooper, making barrels for a firm of distillers.

He attended meetings of a new group called the Sheffield Workingmans' Association. Also the first local chartist group started around this time and Holberry became an active member. The Chartists were so called because they had a list, The People's Charter, of requirements and rights they believed all workers and citizens should have. Almost all of their requirements have now become law.

By 1839 Holberry was heavily involved with and dedicated to their activities. Pawson and Brailsford's Illustrated Guide To Sheffield (1879) describes the events:

*"Meetings and processions were frequent and on the 13th of August that year a street riot occurred and was quelled by the police.....On the 12th September a 'silent' meeting was held in Paradise Square...They also held meetings at Sky Edge, using torchlights."*

On January 11 and 12, 1840, the Chartists tried to take control of the city. They didn't manage it as many of them were betrayed and so caught.

*"Their plans were to seize the Town Hall and the Tontine Hotel (a coaching Inn) as headquarters in the first instance. ...During the evening of the 11th of January, definite information of the plans and designs of the conspirators reached the authorities... Holberry was suddenly and unexpectedly arrested at his house, No 19 Eyre Lane, about midnight."*

Samuel and seven others were sent to York jail to answer charges of high treason on March 16, 1840. This charge held the death penalty, but they were found guilty of the lesser charge of conspiracy and sentenced to four years imprisonment in Northallerton House of Correction. This included some time on a treadmill, and also solitary confinement. Holberry's health failed rapidly and despite appeals for his release he died in York hospital on June 21 1842, aged just 27. His body was returned to Sheffield, with the funeral procession passing from Attercliffe to the then new General Cemetery. 50,000 or so people lined the route. His tombstone can be found down a smaller path off from the front of the Cemetery offices. It bears the inscription

*"Sacred to the memory of Samuel Holberry Who at the early age of 27 died in York Castle, after suffering an imprisonment of two years and three months, June 21st 1842. For advocating what to him appeared to be the true interest of the people of England."*

It lies with those of fellow protesters and his wife. Other words on the tomb reflect his belief in equality for all classes;

*"Vanished is the feverish dream of life, the rich and poor find no distinction here. The great and lowly end their care and strife, The well beloved may have afflictions tear but at the last the oppressor and the slave shall equal stand before the bar of God."*

## Near to the Cemetery

This pagoda style building at the bottom of London Road started life in 1914, as the Lansdowne Picture Palace.

It closed with Blitz damage in 1940, but was repaired. Since then it has had various incarnations as dancehalls, bingo halls and nightclubs.

At present it is a night club and painted a dowdy black, hiding the old stained glass.

The old Lansdowne Cinema during its days as Tiffany's night club

Right is one of the decorations that used to grace the old Co-op building near the city end of Ecclesall Road. The Co-op was demolished and replaced by a Safeways store. One of these coloured ceramic flower vases, which were made by Doulton, used to be on the wall at the store entrance but has now gone. Safeways head office say it has gone to a museum somewhere.

# Wharncliffe Crags

**Between Wortley and Grenoside, at Wharncliffe, is an ancient site. Evidence of settlements and quarry working echo the people who lived and worked there...**

On high ground between Wortley and Grenoside, eight miles north-west of Sheffield City Centre, are Wharncliffe crags. It is a fascinating site, populated for thousands of years. Wharncliffe is one of the largest areas in Europe where quern making activity has been found and investigated. It is this activity that gave the area the name Wharncliffe, deriving from "Quern Cliff" or Qwerncliffe" as it used to be written.

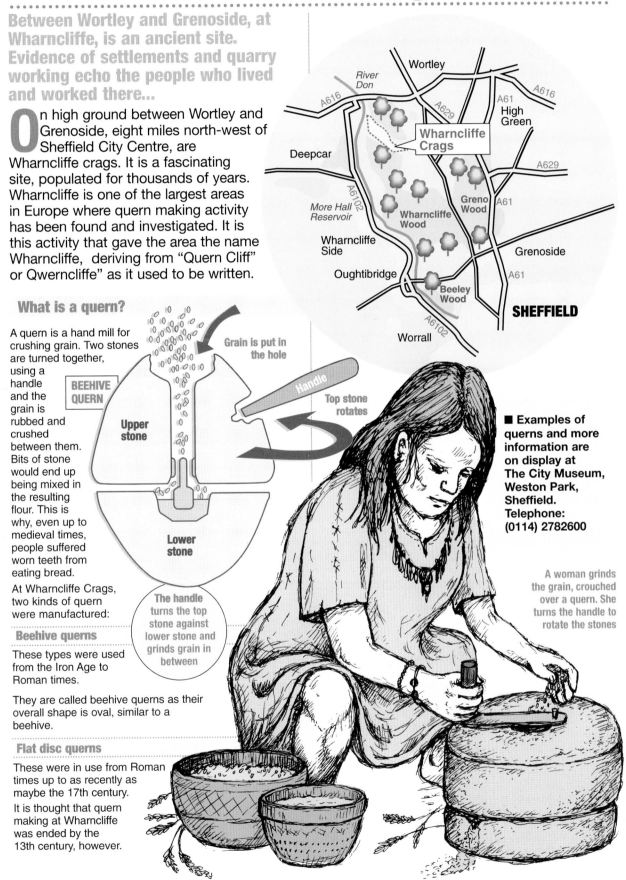

## What is a quern?

A quern is a hand mill for crushing grain. Two stones are turned together, using a handle and the grain is rubbed and crushed between them. Bits of stone would end up being mixed in the resulting flour. This is why, even up to medieval times, people suffered worn teeth from eating bread.

At Wharncliffe Crags, two kinds of quern were manufactured:

### Beehive querns

These types were used from the Iron Age to Roman times.

They are called beehive querns as their overall shape is oval, similar to a beehive.

### Flat disc querns

These were in use from Roman times up to as recently as maybe the 17th century.

It is thought that quern making at Wharncliffe was ended by the 13th century, however.

**BEEHIVE QUERN**

Grain is put in the hole

Handle

Top stone rotates

Upper stone

Lower stone

The handle turns the top stone against lower stone and grinds grain in between

■ Examples of querns and more information are on display at The City Museum, Weston Park, Sheffield. Telephone: (0114) 2782600

*A woman grinds the grain, crouched over a quern. She turns the handle to rotate the stones*

Wortley
River Don
A616
A629
A61
A616
High Green
Deepcar
Wharncliffe Crags
A629
A6102
More Hall Reservoir
Wharncliffe Wood
Greno Wood
A61
Wharncliffe Side
Grenoside
A61
Oughtibridge
Beeley Wood
A6102
SHEFFIELD
Worrall

*"Grey Wharncliffe and the oaks that stand
Like spectres of their sires sublime;
Yet how unlike, though old and grand,
Those giants of the olden time!
Symbols of age-old funerals"..*
Ebeneezer Elliott

PHOTO: SHEFFIELD
NEWSPAPER ARCHIVES

## The Crags

The site covers nearly 200 acres and consists of quarry workings on many different levels, or floors, in the rocks.

The sandstone crags and the many boulders provided the raw material for the querns. The stone is pale grey or golden when freshly broken, weathering to dark grey and has a fine grained texture.

Some unfinished querns are left at the 500 working places. The quern workings were discovered by a local amateur archaeologist, Leslie Butcher, in 1949.

He drew up a detailed survey of the area. In 1996 a fire destroyed some of the vegetation, exposing more querns and working, so English Heritage did a new survey to record these.

Above: a view of the crags. Right: A roughly cut, unfinished quern.

Greno Woods

## A Protected Site

The quern-making area is protected as a Scheduled Ancient Monument and is also designated a Site of Special Scientific Interest, as well as being a RIGS (Regionally Important Geological site).

This means that the area is protected against damage and disturbance. Please respect this if you visit.

Also on the area around the crags are traces of old field systems, and settlement enclosures where the quern makers lived. Excavation in one of these turned up some Romano-British pottery.

In Greno Woods is a triangular enclosure, with a ditch and a bank. There are traces of a building which are probably a medieval forest worker's house.

A beehive (top) and a flat quern

## The Dragon of Wantley

This old legend, found in a book called Percy's Reliques of 1685, and mentioned in Walter Scott's Ivanhoe, is based in the Wharncliffe area, in the time of Elizabeth 1. It is in the form of a bawdy poem, and the name Wantley is probably a composite word made up of the names Wharncliffe and Wortley.

The tale concerns a dreadful dragon, living on the crags:

*"This dragon had two furious wings.*
*Each one upon his shoulder;*
*With a sting in his tail,*
*as long as a flail,*
*He had long claws, in his paws*
*Four and forty teeth of iron"*

*"All sorts of cattle this dragon did eat,*
*Some say he ate up trees;*
*And that the forest sure he would*
*Devour by degrees"*

The people approached More, a brave and virile local knight, from nearby More Hall, and asked him to rid them of the dragon. He said he would do so if he could have a dark haired, fair skinned damsel to 'anoint and dress him for battle'. This was agreed and More went to Sheffield to have armour covered in spikes made.

*"Had you but seen him in his dress,*
*how fierce he looked and big*
*You would of thought him to have been*
*Some Egyptian porcupig"*

The next day, he arose late and strangely weary from his damsel and was invigorated with six pots of ale. He then sneakily hid in a well where the dragon was known to drink.

When the dragon came he leapt out and hit it, taking it totally by surprise as it quenched its thirst.

One of the dragon's weapons seemed to be flatulence, which it used to the full after this unexpected assault!

*"Oh! Quoth the Dragon,*
*Pox take you, come out,*
*You that disturbed me in my drink,*
*With that he turned and fharted at him,*
*Good ask, how he did stink!*
*Beeshrew my soul, thy body is foul,*
*Thy dung smells not like balsam"*

Two and a half days later they still fought, the knight's spiny armour and the dragons scales protecting them both. The battle was eventually won when More attacked the dragon's only vulnerable spot and kicked it up the bottom with his pointy metal boot. The dragon then turned around six times and died, with a final flatulent flair. Reminders from the legend can be found around the area. There is a Dragon's Well and a Dragon's Den marked on the ordnance Survey map of the area, near Wharncliffe Lodge. Also the coat of arms of the More family(right) bears a green dragon. Some think the legend is an allegory about feuding landlords, More of More Hall and his neighbour and rival, from Wortley Hall. On nearby Bradfield Church, one of the carvings on the exterior is of a dragon, maybe recalling the legend. Also, in the foyer of the Town Hall on Pinstone Street is a carving said to show the Knight and Dragon from this local tale and not St George and his dragon as many could think.

## Mystery Stone

On a stone in Wharncliffe wood, just down the railway line from Wardsend Cemetery, is a carving of an American Indian head, complete with feathered head-dress.

Some thought the rock, two feet high by about a foot wide, was to mark the grave of Lone Wolf, a performer in Buffalo Bill's Wild West show that visited the city around 1860, staying at Penistone Road. But Lone Wolf, who died from 'flu whilst travelling with the show in 1892, was in fact buried in London. More recently, in September 1992, his family came to take his remains back to the United States.

Author Alan Gallop, in his book Buffalo Bill's British Wild West, mentions a young indian brave, Paul Eagle Star, who lost his foot in a riding accident at the circus and sadly died of gangrene shortly after. "News of his untimely death has cast a deep gloom over the encampment", reported The Star. Could the stone be in his memory?

The truth and the carver of the stone remain a mystery.

The carved stone in Wharncliffe Wood

PHOTO: SHEFFIELD NEWSPAPERS

# Wharncliffe Heath

## The Nature Reserve

**Around the crags is an area of heathland, the Wharncliffe Heath Nature Reserve.**

**This is a site for the protection of many kinds of wildlife. It is situated above Wharncliffe Crags and overlooks Deepcar and Stocksbridge.**

The clearing of the area is thought to have begun when the earliest quern workings began, about 7,500 years ago. The area was designated a County Nature Reserve in October 1995, The northern section of the heath is referred to as Long Heath on 19th century maps so may be very old.

The rocks were exposed for working by burning sections of the heath.

The southern section was originally called Haystack Copy (Coppice).

Birch trees in this area probably provided fuel for the local smelting industry.

Before the electrification of the nearby railway line in the 1950's, there were many fires caused in the area by passing steam trains.

This gave continuity to the nature of the area as open heathland by burning the growth periodically.

## Vegetation

The area is covered in heather, bracken and birch, with tufted hair grass, purple moor grass and rushes in the sections in the wet sections with less drainage.

On the eastern side of the heath is a strip of woodland, which is around 50 years old, with an area of birch and oak trees. The northern end of the heath has mature oak, birch and sycamore woodland.

Hundreds of other plants and shrubs are found on the heath, including bugle, angelica, broom, mugwort, foxglove, St. Johns Wort, ox-eye daisy, wild parsnip, figwort, ragwort, goldenrod and marsh violet.

PHOTO: COURTESY OF SWAP

## Wildlife

The Nature Reserve is home to many species of birds, including the White Throat, Tree Pipit, Willow Warbler, Yellow Hammer, Linnet and Woodcock.

Mammals include the above mentioned red deer. In summer a herd of Hebridean Sheep graze the area.

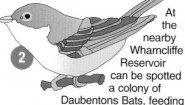

At the nearby Wharncliffe Reservoir can be spotted a colony of Daubentons Bats, feeding above the pond on the site. Common lizards and grass snake have also been spotted in the area, as well as a regionally important colony of Palmate Newt, common toad and common frog in the large pond in the north east corner of the reserve.

Here can also be found Common Hawker Dragonfly Nymph and Green Tiger Beetles.

1. Oak leaves
2. Whitethroat (female)
3. Yellowhammer (male)
4. Palmate Newt
5. Green Tiger Beetle
6. Foxglove

**Further Details:**

■ If you would like to find out more about the reserve, the work of the Yorkshire Wildlife Trust or Sheffield Wildlife Action Partnership, contact SWAP, Parks, Woodlands and Countryside Division, Brook Road, Meersbrook, Sheffield S8 9FL

Telephone: (0114) 250 0500

# Conisbrough Castle

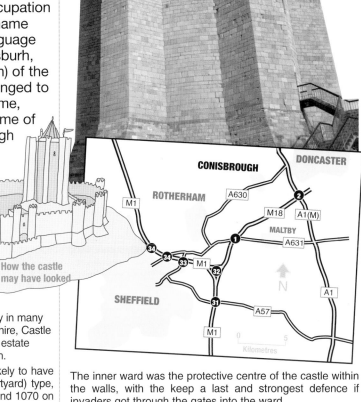

The splendid Norman Keep of Conisbrough Castle

**Looking proudly over the rooftops of Conisbrough are the remains of an ancient castle. At the heart of these ruins stands what is considered to be the finest Norman Keep in the country...**

Conisbrough has been a site of occupation since well before its Castle. The name comes from the Anglo-Saxon language and their name for the town- Cyningesburh, which means 'the defended burh (town) of the King'. This suggests that the area belonged to one of the Anglo-Saxon kings of the time, before the Norman Conquest. At the time of the conquest, the manor of Conisbrough was held by King Harold, who was defeated in the Battle of Hastings.

## Builders of the Castle

After the Norman invasion of 1066, the occupiers set about establishing their force with many strong castles. One of the Norman King William's original men and chief knights from Normandy was William, the first Earl Warenne, his son-in-law. The King gave him property in many areas of England, the biggest estates being in Yorkshire, Castle Acre in Norfolk and Lewes in Sussex. The Yorkshire estate seems to have been biggest, centred at Conisbrough.

How the castle may have looked

The castle that Earl William built in the town was likely to have been the motte (mound) and bailey (enclosed courtyard) type, but little is known about it. It was probably built around 1070 on the site of the present stone castle. In 1088 Earl William died of battle wounds. He was succeeded by the second Earl, his son William, who was Earl until 1138.

The third Earl, again called William, succeeded in 1138 until his death at the Crusades in 1147. He left a daughter, Isabel, who married the son of King Stephen, William de Blois, who became the fourth Earl Warenne. He died without an heir in 1159 and King Henry II re-married Isabel off in 1163 to Hamelin Plantagenet, his half brother.

## The Keep

Hamelin, fifth Earl, held the earldom until his death in 1202 and it was during this time that the great stone keep was built. It is 90ft high, with walls 15ft thick in parts. The cylindrical design makes it the only one of its kind in the country. The nearest in style is at Mortemer, near Dieppe, France, a castle also held by the Warenne family. The second floor (Lord's Hall), has a grand fireplace and the third floor has a fine private chapel. Soon after the 'curtain' surrounding walls were built, with more buildings added probably by Hamelin's son, William, Earl from 1202 to 1239.

The Keep chapel

The inner ward was the protective centre of the castle within the walls, with the keep a last and strongest defence if invaders got through the gates into the ward.

The castle passed through descendants of the family until the eighth Earl, John, in 1304. He had a skirmish with Thomas, the Earl of Lancaster. As a result, Thomas laid siege to and seized Conisbrough in 1317. His end came in 1322, after he led a rebellion against King Edward II, ending in the battle of Boroughbridge. The King won, and Thomas was executed outside his own castle at Pontefract.

After this Edward II held Conisbrough until 1326 and stayed there briefly in November 1322. In 1324 he ordered repairs to the castle, which was given back to the eight Earl John de Warenne, in 1326. After John's death, without heirs, the castle was owned by the crown again.

Peeks at the Past

## KEY

1. **12th century Keep**
2. **Stairs**
3. **Kitchen**
4. **Bakehouse**
5. **Service Area**
6. **Buttery** (wine & ale store)
7. **Great Hall** (communal)
8. **West Range**
9. **Great Chamber** (above)
10. **Barbican** (to protect gate)
11. **Prison** (below ground)
12. **Gatehouse**
13. **Chapel** (possibly)
14. **Fallen wall**
15. **Inner Ward**

A simplified plan of the castle

Modern stair on line of old ones

Collapsed wall

Metres
0  10  20  30

Feet
0  20  40  60  80  90

A bird's eye view of the Castle
PHOTO: DENNIS LOUND

Adding atmosphere to renovated Castle rooms, with replica furniture and moody lighting

## The Castle neglected

In 1537, a survey of the castle was carried out for Henry VIII. It showed the castle had been neglected badly, with gates, bridge and stonework fallen, as well as one of the floors of the keep being collapsed. 60ft of the south wall, including the main gate with portcullis and drawbridge, had fallen by then, probably from subsidence. The remains of the castle were granted by Henry VIII to the Carey family.

The early damage, rendering the castle useless as a defence, meant that in the Civil War of the 17th century, the troops didn't bother damaging it further, so it is relatively undamaged today. It was purchased by the local council in the late 1940's and is now owned by English Heritage. A new roof and floors have been built and a new visitor centre.

## Ivanhoe

*"There are few more beautiful or striking scenes in England, than are presented by the vicinity of this ancient Saxon fortress. The soft and gentle river Don sweeps through an amphitheatre... and on a mount, ascending from the river, well defended by by walls and ditches, rises this ancient edifice... a royal residence of the Kings of England."*  IVANHOE

The fame of Conisbrough Castle was spread by Sir Walter Scott, in his novel Ivanhoe, though he calls it a 'Saxon Fortress'. The tales in the book of the reign of Richard I are fictitious. By then the keep would just have been built, but the castle would not then have had the enclosing stone walls.

Conisbrough Castle is managed by the **Ivanhoe Trust** on behalf of **English Heritage & Doncaster Metropolitan Borough Council.** There is an entrance fee.

Opening Times are: 10 - 5 every day (30 April-1st Oct) 10 - 4 rest of the year.

For further information, special rates, etc. please contact Conisbrough Castle Visitor Centre on **01709 863329,** Fax no: **01709 866773.**
www.conisbrough castle.org.uk

48

## St. Peter's Church, Conisbrough

### An ancient site of worship

There is strong evidence to suggest this historic church dates from 1250 years ago, pre-dating Conisbrough Castle by about 400 years, though there may well have been an earlier church, made of wood, on the same site.

Before this there was probably a simple preaching cross, which served as a point around which people would gather for worship. Weathered remains of this stone cross can be seen in the graveyard. The present church is a mixture of architectural styles, built upon over the years.

In Saxon times the church was probably a Minster (mother church) to several other churches in the area. When it was built in 750 AD it was much smaller than it is today.

The original entrance of this church was where the south side of the tower is, now inside the building after it was widened in later years. Then the tower was a two storey porch.

On either side of the nave were small side extensions called a Porticus. These had two storeys, and the priest is thought to have lived in the upper rooms.

By 1050 AD the chancel of the church had been enlarged.

When the castle was built, the people moving into the area needed a much bigger church and it is believed that Hamelin Plantagenet, the builder of the Norman castle, also had the church enlarged between 1150 and 1200AD. Arches were cut into the original Saxon walls and with the larger surrounding walls formed narrow side aisles. A new entrance doorway was created, which is the one there today, inside the entrance porch.

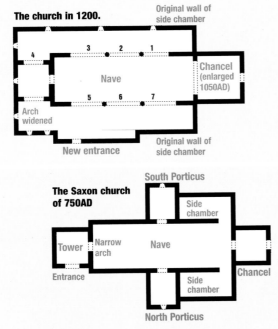

The church in 1200.

Original wall of side chamber

Nave

Chancel (enlarged 1050AD)

Arch widened

New entrance

Original wall of side chamber

South Porticus

The Saxon church of 750AD

Side chamber

Tower | Narrow arch | Nave

Entrance

Chancel

Side chamber

North Porticus

PHOTO: STAR NEWSPAPER

Over the road, close to the Castle, lies St.Peter's, the oldest church in South Yorkshire, and still very much in use.

Building the arches took a long time, with building spreading in three phases over 50 years or so. In this time architectural fashion had changed. This can be seen in the different arch shapes. The earliest ones are rounded arches and the last ones to be built are in the more pointed style which was by then the new fad.

Around then the tower was heightened and the roof renewed.

More changes ensued in the 13th 14th and 15th centuries. In 1475 three bells were added, raising the tower again. Alterations of the 16th 17th and 18th century were wiped out by a 'restoration' in 1866.

In the 17th century the Puritan Iconoclasts, against graven images, knocked heads off some of the pillar carvings.

Other features in the church include the **squint** in the NE pillar of the nave, which allowed people to see the priest performing communion. In the 15th century the altar was moved back so it was no longer any use. There are also some splendid carved stones: an ornate 12th century **tomb chest** with knights, zodiac signs and a dragon and **another tomb chest** with birds. Opposite the entrance are some **13th century windows**, with glass added later. Other fine glass is found in the church. Some of the pews have wooden **mice** carved on their ends.

■ There are guided tours of the church every Sunday afternoon at 2.30pm. **Services: Sundays at 9.30, 11.15, 6.30 and 8.30** Phone 01709 867718 for further details.

# Around Portobello

**Just off West Street is an area known as Portobello. Around here are many historic connections, including a hospital, a relish factory and Samuel Plimsoll's early home.**

The Jessop Hospital for Women was founded by Thomas Jessop in 1878, to replace an earlier hospital at Figtree Lane, which had been founded in 1864.

## Thomas Jessop

Jessop was born on 31 January 1804, in Blast Lane, Sheffield, into a family of crucible steel makers. When his brother died he took over the family business. The works, at Brightside, became one of the biggest in the country.

Jessop became a well known local figure, and became Master Cutler in 1863 as well as mayor in 1863.

He used part of his fortune to help build a new hospital for women. The building that housed the old hospital at Figtree Lane is still there and has the plaque shown far right to identify it. He gave the building costs for the new building at Leavygreave Road, almost £30,000.

The Jessop Hospital at Leavy Greave Road - an old print

The Figtree Lane hospital - an old print

The hospital is described in that oft quoted Pawson and Brailsford Illustrated Guide to Sheffield of 1879...

*"The new hospital was formally opened by Mr Jessop in July of last year. It is divided into two parts - one for the treatment of disease and the other for midwifery..... The style is Tudor freely treated, the architect, Mr J.D.Webster, having introduced with very good effect certain Burgundian*

An ornate door frame at the Jessop Hospital

Above: An imposing portrait of Mr Thomas Jessop, which now hangs at the Cutlers' Hall

Jessop died on 30 November 1887 and is buried in Ecclesall Parish church. The Jessop Hospital has now moved to its new home just behind the Hallamshire Hospital.

The old Jessop Hospital site at Leavy Greave Road is partly awaiting its fate and partly used by the University.

IN THIS BUILDING THE ORIGINAL
SHEFFIELD HOSPITAL FOR WOMEN
WAS FOUNDED WITH 6 BEDS
ON 29TH JUNE 1864.
TRANSFERRED TO LEAVYGREAVE ROAD
AS THE
JESSOP HOSPITAL FOR WOMEN
ON 22ND JULY 1878.

The plaque on the first hospital for women at Figtree Lane

PHOTO: SHEFFIELD NEWSPAPERS

Jessop's in the 1950's

## A musical memorial

In the nearby graveyard of St George's church can be found a tomb with music carved upon it. The tomb, at the corner nearest the junction of St George's Terrace and Brook Hill, is the resting place of Benjamin Coldwell, who owned a lime and plaster works and died in 1868. He had a library which he opened to the public, The music and words on the stone (shown below) are of his favourite hymn.

*"Great God! What do I see here! The end of things created!"*

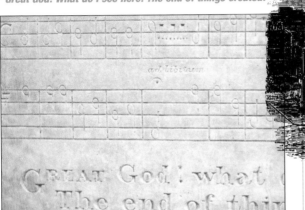

St George's Church

The carvings, left, are on the Mappin Institute for the Blind, Mappin Street. They are by artist Philip Lindsay Clark, in 1938. Clark also did carvings on the old gas showrooms on Commercial Street.

Look out for this interesting sign for W E Harrison at Regents Terrace as you wander the area, it bears the proud claim 'Steeplejack of Nelson Column fame'. This old firm was established in 1854 and is still in business just a little way up the same Terrace. The Nelson Column connection comes from the fact that one of the Harrison family climbed the column in 1896 to decorate it with flowers and check it over.

## Henderson's Relish

Opposite the original doorway of the hospital on Leavy Greave Road, can be found the Henderson's Relish factory. This famous Sheffield Institution was started by a Mr Henry Henderson. He began making his own special brand of sauce in the late 19th century.

The factory was originally at 35 Broad Lane, Sheffield. The factory today is still in full swing, less than half a mile from this original site, on Leavy Greave Road. This has been the home of Henderson's since 1960.

Known fondly locally as 'Hendo's' the relish is rather like Worcester sauce in appearance but with a different flavour that includes tamarinds, cloves and cayenne pepper made to a secret recipe. It is used on many foods, including meat dishes and fish and chips.

The trademark bright orange label is sometimes changed for special editions. The fame of this local delicacy has spread far and wide and many ex-pats say they miss it, or request bottles from their relatives in Sheffield.

As well as the relish, the company now make 'Desperate Dan's Spicy Tomato Splash', named after the pie loving Beano character and aimed at the children's market.

The factory is tiny and full of character and though rumours of a move keep surfacing, the company are still in these unassuming premises. Over 15,000 bottles a week are produced here.

The Hendersons factory

Many famous people are fans of Henderson's Relish, including Sean Bean and Peter Stringfellow.

The factory is at Hendersons Ltd, Leavygreave Road, Sheffield S3 7RA

tel (0114) 272 5909

e mail: sales@hendersons-relish.co.uk

web site: www.hendersons-relish.co.uk

## Samuel Plimsoll (1824-1898)

**Samuel Plimsoll, who invented the Plimsoll line used on ships, used to live in the Portobello area of Sheffield. Plimsoll was concerned that many ships were overloaded and would probably sink in a rough sea. This did not concern the ship owners, who knew they could claim insurance on their lost cargo and did not stop to worry about the loss of life that was likely too.**

Plimsoll was born on February 10, 1824, in Bristol. He was the son of Thomas and Priscilla. The family moved from Bristol to Penrith in 1828, then in 1838 to Sheffield. Samuel left school at 15 and worked for a Sheffield Solicitor, then at The People's College in 1842. The family were living in Regent Street at this time. There is a plaque on the building which now stands opposite the site of his old home.

In 1851 Samuel acted as honorary secretary for the Great Exhibition in London and selected exhibits from Sheffield.

In 1853 he moved to London to try his luck as a coal merchant, but ended up bankrupt and by early 1855 he was back in Sheffield.

He had always had an interest in improving the lot of the working man, and supported the unions' work for healthier conditions. He helped with relief funds for mining accidents and became known in South Yorkshire as The Miner's friend. He was angered by the loss of life in shipping and came up with the idea of a safe mark for the loading of ships, showing when they were taking the maximum weight. He felt that many ships were overinsured, undermanned and overloaded and he campaigned for better standards. He also published Cattle Ships, which denounced cruelty to animals, as well as pamphlets on the coal trade amongst other essays and was active in running for political seats in Liverpool and Sheffield

He married Eliza Ann Railton from Chapeltown in 1857 at Ecclesfield Parish Church. From 1865 they lived at Whiteley Wood Hall. Their only child Eliza died young and is said to be buried in Fulwood chapel (Samuel's wife Eliza died in 1882. He married second wife Harriet Frankish Wade Hull in 1885).

In 1868 Samuel allowed miners to have their annual procession in the grounds of Whitely Wood Hall as they were not allowed in the usual spot of Norfolk Park. He made a speech supporting trade unions and appeared on some of their banners, including that of the national Amalgamated Sailors and Fireman's Union. (see Banner Bright by John Gorman, 1973, ISBN 0 7139 0290, 6 page 109).

In 1869, Samuel saw an article in the Sheffield Telegraph about the loss of life of fishermen in poorly designed trawlers.

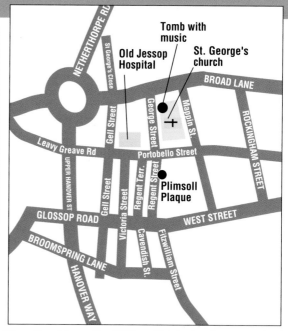

Plimsoll met the editor, William Christopher Leng, who had written it, recognising a like mind.

Leng had also campaigned against so called 'coffin ships' and encouraged Plimsoll to become more involved in fighting for better conditions and safety, with the backing of the newspaper. In 1870 Samuel Plimsoll began his load line campaign. In 1872 he published an attack on shipowners called 'Our Seamen', as well as bills for reform.

He caused a scene in The House of Commons with his outspoken views. Public attention was gained by this and helped with the passing of an act that became The Merchant Shipping Act. The Merchant Shipping Act was given final amendments in 1876. This act obliged owners to mark the side of every ship with his load lines, a circular disc and a horizontal line drawn through the centre (the Plimsoll Line), indicating to what depth a ship may be loaded. This Plimsoll Line earned him the nickname 'The Sailor's Friend.'

The same year as the Plimsoll Line became law, 1876, a new type of canvas shoe with rubber strengthening was marketed and named a 'Plimsoll' in his honour. The name is said to have been coined by a sales rep from the Liverpool rubber company who said the rubber band reminded him of the Plimsoll Line. The shoes are water tight as long as the water is kept below the rubber line.

After a long illness Samuel Plimsoll died at Folkestone in 1898, where he had resided for some years.

**A Plimsoll line on the side of a ship**

A bronze bust of Samuel Plimsoll (shown left), stands on Victoria Embankment in London, in between Horseguards Avenue and Whitehall Place. Erected in 1929, it has a bust of Plimsoll and below him is a ship and a tablet with small statues of a sailor on either side of him. The fence around it has Plimsoll lines as decoration (right) The inscription reads:

*"Samuel Plimsoll, Born 1824, died 1898. Erected by Members of the National Union of Seamen in grateful recognition of his services to the men of the sea of all nations."*

# Sheffield Castle

How the castle may have looked, a drawing by Martin Davenport

In the cellars of the aptly named Castle Market are found all that remains of the city's once proud castle. One time prison of Mary Queen of Scots, it was destroyed by Parliamentarians in the Civil War of 1647.

Sheffield Castle stood by the Rivers Don and Sheaf, its other sides defended by a water filled moat. The moat was crossed by a drawbridge, and the castle entered beneath two towers.

## Around the castle

The first castle was built around 1150AD by a Norman baron from Huntingdonshire, called William de Lovetot. There was a motte (mound) and a bailey (outer wall). In the inner bailey was the main castle, on top of a mound, later known as Castle Hill. This was the stronghold of the Lord of the Manor. A defensive ditch was dug around it, and the resulting earth was used to make the mound in the centre. This original castle was burned down by rioting barons and a new stone one was built in 1270 by Thomas de Furnival. Because of the rivers, a moat was only needed around a small part of the castle. To make the moat, ditches were built at what are now Exchange Street and Waingate and the rivers were allowed to flow into them.

Waingate was the old wagon road into Sheffield. Wain is an old name for wagon, (as in Constable's Haywain). At the side of this road was the Castle Green, which some people think was a tournament ground. At the top of Castle Green was an open sewer, called Truelove's Gutter, hardly romantic, which was named after a local family.

Nearby were built a hospital and a corn mill, at the nearby area still called Millsands. Also around here was an area called the Bullstake. Here, in part of the old market area, bulls were baited by dogs, beasts were sold and a town bull may have stood for hire. Beyond this area were orchards and Sheffield Park, which in 1637 covered 2,460 acres. Here deer were chased for sport by the Lord of the Manor's hunting party. The park was also full of huge oak trees. The castle lasted until 1648, when it was demolished by order of Parliament.

## A Royal Prison

Between 1570 and 1584, Sheffield Castle was one of the prisons for Mary Queen of Scots, along with 30 of her attendants. Queen Elizabeth 1 had ordered the Lord of the Manor, George Talbot, the 6th Earl of Shrewsbury, to contain her there. Mary was a political embarrassment so the Queen sent her away to Yorkshire out of the way.

She was commended to the care of George, 6th Earl of Shrewsbury and arrived at his castle residence in Sheffield on 28th November 1570. It was a hard thing accommodating and upkeeping the Queen and her retinue, so she was moved around to various houses, probably to spread the cost as well as make her harder to find!

She was held in this area for over 13 years, with stays at the castle, Sheffield Manor and Chatsworth. She then moved to Wingfield, then Tutbury, then Chartley in Staffordshire.

Left: Mary Queen of Scots

### The Babbington Plot

A Norton youth called Anthony Babbington, heir to a large Derbyshire estate, had been Mary's page since she had arrived at Sheffield Castle. He was sympathetic to her cause and in 1586 he helped her plot a Catholic insurrection, to release Mary and kill Queen Elizabeth and her ministers. Somehow Elizabeth got hold of letters containing details of the plot and all the conspirators were hanged. Mary herself was brought to trial for treason, condemned and put to death by beheading at Fothergay Castle on 8th February 1587.

### The Stones remain

Some stones from the castle are to be seen under the Castle Market. They can be visited by appointment on Thursdays between 9am and 3pm by telephoning the Markets Customer Information Centre on (0114) 2736245.

In late 2001, there was an archeological dig at the site of Sheffield Castle. ARCUS, a consultancy at the University of Sheffield, now believe that much more of the castle has survived than was first thought. 600 year old floor tiles and glass were discovered during the dig, as well as much more of the structure. It is hoped this can be a feature of any future developments in the area.

Some of the castle stones that remain, under the Castle Market.

# Sheffield Manor

**This old manor house, the ruins of which remain and give the Manor Estate its name, began life as a medieval hunting lodge for the gentry out hunting deer in Sheffield Park.**

The Lodge was built by George, the fourth Earl of Shrewsbury in 1516, though there had been earlier buildings on the site. The original lodge was oblong, with two large courtyards. It is often mistakenly referred to as "Manor Castle." In the 16th century, it was enlarged to be a splendid residence, for the Earl of Shrewsbury to use as an alternative lodging to the castle. In 1529, Cardinal Wolsey, in disgrace with Henry VIII, stayed at the Manor as a guest of the Earl of Shrewsbury.

## Custody of Mary

As well as being held in the castle, Mary Queen of Scots was held as an unwilling 'guest' at the Sheffield Manor. This may have been a reason for enlarging and improving the place, so it was fit for a royal personage.

The Turret House

Many people thought the Turret or Gate House, the only part of the manor left with a roof, was where Mary was kept. This is unlikely as it is very small and Mary probably had a suite of rooms to fit in herself and all her attendants in the much more luxurious Manor itself. The Turret House was also at the edge of the manor, near the main gate, not a very secure place to hold such an important prisoner. Built in 1574, the likelihood is that it was a gatehouse, perhaps used as a small hunting lodge, which were very popular then. There are still some original features to see inside, including fine plasterwork.

In 1708, the 8th Duke of Norfolk ordered part of Manor Lodge to be demolished and sold the materials. A great gale in 1793 blew down one of the two remaining towers and the bricks and stonework were taken by locals to use in their house building. The Turret House was restored in the 1870's by the Duke of Norfolk of the time. In 1907 the ruins were fenced off and left until 1953, when the site was leased to Sheffield Corporation to help preserve it. Now local groups Friends of Manor 'Castle', Manor & Castle Development Trust and Sheffield Wildlife Trust also work to help secure the historic site's future.

## Secret tunnels

Local stories of secret tunnels from Sheffield Castle are rife. It is said that Mary Queen of Scots walked from here to Sheffield Manor, escorted by guards. Tales of her treading a path beneath the city to mass at Sheffield Cathedral and of a tunnel from Sheffield Manor to Woodhouse are also common. It is now thought by local group Friends of Manor Castle however, that the tunnel may have been invented after people had seen a much less romantic drain for the toilet, which looked like a tunnel. This too is now gone.

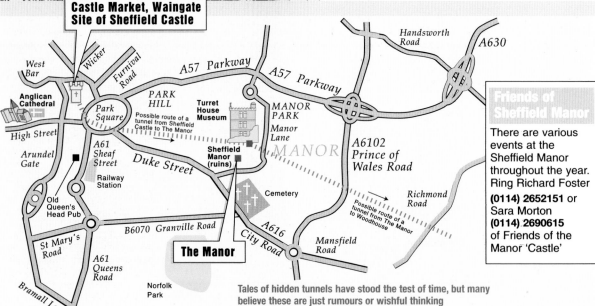

**Friends of Sheffield Manor**

There are various events at the Sheffield Manor throughout the year. Ring Richard Foster **(0114) 2652151** or Sara Morton **(0114) 2690615** of Friends of the Manor 'Castle'

Tales of hidden tunnels have stood the test of time, but many believe these are just rumours or wishful thinking

# Wincobank Hill

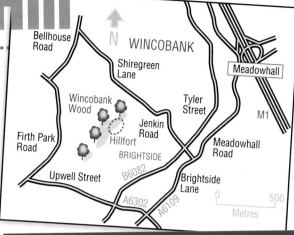

**Two and a half miles to the north-east of the centre of Sheffield sits one of the most impressive and little mentioned monuments in the area.**

Just over 160 metres high and steep, Wincobank Hill can be seen for miles, especially to the South East in the Don and Rother Valleys, where the land is flat or low. This gives the place an air of command and mystery, like Glastonbury Tor in Somerset, as well as making it an excellent position for defence. These reasons mean that for centuries, the site has been an important one.

## Why is it there?

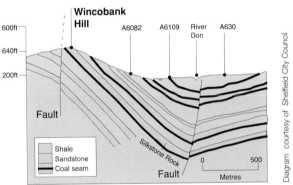

*Diagram courtesy of Sheffield City Council*

If approached from the Grimesthorpe direction, it is easy to see sandstone exposed at the surface at the top of the hill. From the hill, the land dips into a line or FAULT. The rocks here, shales and coal seams as well as the sandstone, dip deeply towards this fault then become relatively level again. This kind of land feature is called a MONOCLINE. The highest part of the hill is where a layer of land known as the Silkstone Rock is at the surface. Because this has eroded more slowly it has resulted in a narrow, hogsback shaped hill, which slopes away steeply to the North West (Firth Park and Shiregreen) and the South-East (towards Lower Don Valley). This hogsback hill has been cut through to the North-East by Blackburn Brook at Meadowhall and to the South West by a minor stream at Grimesthorpe, so it also slopes steeply in those directions. This has left a dry, easily defended hilltop with all-round views, a very desirable location for many people in prehistory.

## The Iron Age Hillfort

At the summit of the hill is Wincobank hillfort. This ancient site consists of an oval, defensive enclosure, 450ft x 309ft, covering just over 2.5 acres. This is surrounded by a single rampart wall with an external ditch.

The earth and debris thrown up from digging the ditch has been piled up to make an outer bank. The rampart is 2.8 metres at it's highest point. Today it is covered in grass, but still complete except for three breaks. One of these is a very old established track called Wincobank Wood lane.

### ❶ The Ditch

Most of the ditch and outer bank have disappeared. There is an entrance on the north-east side, where one end of the main bank is thickened and the other end runs out across it for 30ft, to form a type of out turned entrance. The original depth of the ditch was 5 - 6 ft

### ❷ The Rampart

In 1899, the site was excavated by E. Howarth, who found the 18ft thick stone rampart. later excavations in 1979 by Sheffield City Museums added more information. Two rows of stones were infilled with earth and sandstone rubble and bonded together by timbers.

The inner side stones were small, unmortared, dressed stones. The outer side was made up of much larger stones. It is hard to judge how high the wall would have been, but it would probably have had a wooden fence, or palisade, on top.

During the rampart excavations, charred timbers were found. In the rubble core the stones had been partly melted by intense heat. This suggests that the rampart was destroyed by fire, accidentally or otherwise. Using the technique of radio carbon dating, charcoal from these burnt timbers was examined.

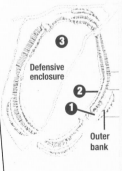

The date this arrived at was around 500BC. This means that the rampart was built in the middle of the Iron Age. Extra protection may have been needed by the people living there as neighbouring communities tried to take control of the Don Valley.

### ❸ Inside the fort

No excavations have been made, so any remnants of post holes from buildings or other signs of occupation have ever been discovered.

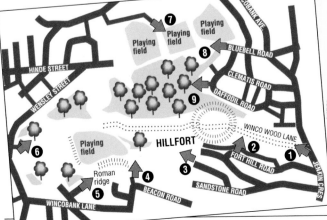

Peeks at the Past

## Who has lived there?

There is evidence that the hilltop had been frequented at a much earlier date than the Iron Age and was also still very important much later. The earliest finds have been Mesolithic (Middle Stone Age) and flint tools (8000 - 3000 BC) have been found.

### The Romans

Later, it is thought that the hillfort was occupied during Roman times, to check the advance of the Roman Armies. The Romans built their own fort facing Wincobank on the opposite side of the Don, two miles away at Templeborough. Brough is the Roman word for fort.

### Other signs of occupation in the area

Down the hill towards the Don Valley are the remains of another earthwork called the Roman Ridge.

This consists of a bank and ditch stretching with breaks for almost 10 miles along the northern side of the Don Valley as far as Mexbrough.

This earthwork was thought to be prehistoric, and built at the same time as Wincobank hillfort. Some believe it was built later, in the Dark Ages, between 450-600AD after the collapse of the Roman Empire, maybe to defend the area from the advancing Anglo Saxons. If this is so, then they most certainly used the hillfort.

The only dating of the ridge so far has been from a 19th century record of a hoard of Roman coins that were apparently found in the ditch.

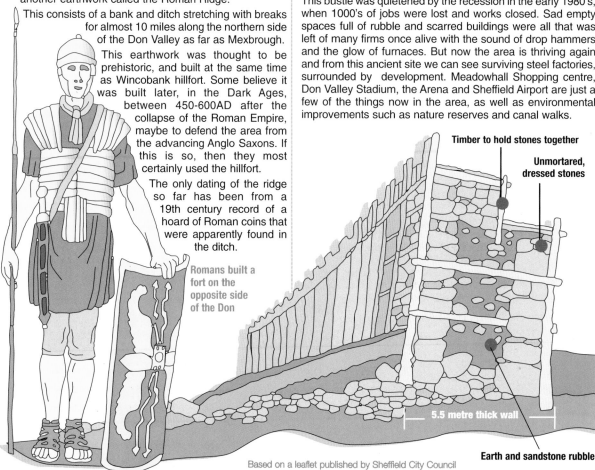

Romans built a fort on the opposite side of the Don

Based on a leaflet published by Sheffield City Council

## Walking on Wincobank Hill

There are many paths up on to the hill, a welcome green space in the city offering wonderful views. Until the middle of the nineteenth century the area was mainly rural, with settlements in Brightside, Attercliffe and Tinsley, parted from Sheffield by fields and woodlands. Later this became the industrial heartland of the area, with canals, railways, steelworks and factories spreading. Flat land and the river made it an ideal place for these developments and houses for the workers sprung up too. Wartime and more industrial expansion in the 1950's meant the specialist steel industry was thriving and the area was constantly busy.

## New horizons

This bustle was quietened by the recession in the early 1980's, when 1000's of jobs were lost and works closed. Sad empty spaces full of rubble and scarred buildings were all that was left of many firms once alive with the sound of drop hammers and the glow of furnaces. But now the area is thriving again and from this ancient site we can see surviving steel factories, surrounded by development. Meadowhall Shopping centre, Don Valley Stadium, the Arena and Sheffield Airport are just a few of the things now in the area, as well as environmental improvements such as nature reserves and canal walks.

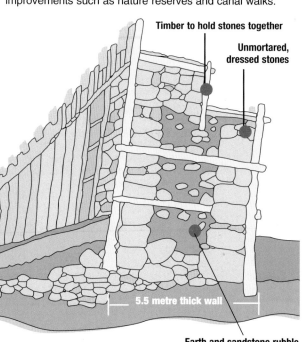

Timber to hold stones together

Unmortared, dressed stones

5.5 metre thick wall

Earth and sandstone rubble

## Wincobank 'Castle'

This old house was really called Parkin Jepson Tower, but it is probably better known by many locals as 'Wincobank Castle'- so nicknamed because of the castle like tower top.

It stood near the summit of Wincobank Hill, and according to local writer J E Vickers, was built by George Parkin between 1887 and 1907. Visitors could climb to the top of the tower if they paid a penny. It was used as an ARP observation post in the first and second World Wars.

The house was demolished in 1960 because it was falling into ruin. Now it is as lost as the other stones on the hill, and Mr Parkin is one of the ghosts of the old place, rubbing shoulders with centurions.

## The old guns

Many a local child played on the old concrete remains of gun turrets. These were at the summit of Wincobank Hill, where they commanded a splendid view of the skies in both World Wars for the gunners.

Zeppelins also flew over this area in 1915. Women and children fell victims to one at nearby Effingham Road, where a plaque bears witness to their memory.

No parts of the guns remains now. The only reminder of the importance of the site in the war is a stone pathway once used by the military vehicles. Stone dual lines lead up to nothing but the rounded shadow of the old hill fort ramparts hidden under the grass.

Any parts of the concrete gun mounts are long gone too - as the site has been made greener for children to play on. They run on grass that covers centuries of history.

# Bryward House

On Commercial Street, in Sheffield City Centre, stand the offices and showrooms of the old United Gas Light Company.

**Close up of one of the Atlantes**

An old print of the Gas Company Offices, from Pawson and Brailsford

## Stone Giants on Commercial Street

Built in 1874, these splendid old buildings were commissioned as the offices of the Sheffield United Gas Light Company. The architects were Hadfield and Son. They are built in the style of a grand villa, with ornate plaster work and fireplaces inside. The general office has a glazed dome. The two large male figures, (Atlantes) around the doorway were made by artist Thomas Earp in 1874. They have foliage instead of legs, with a shell above their heads, and are almost suggestive of sea gods.

There are also ornate panels with foliage and gryphons on the building.

The gas board moved to new premises in the early 1970's and the offices, though enjoying various flings at life including as a cafe, were eventually left to get into bad repair. Now the offices have been rescued and revamped and are awaiting another new owner.

**Right: an old advert for the Gas Co.**

**Above: Sheffield Gas Co. Initials from the top of the building**

THE SHEFFIELD
UNITED GAS LIGHT COMPANY,
GAS FITTERS.

DWELLING-HOUSES, MANUFACTORIES AND PUBLIC BUILDINGS SUPPLIED AND FITTED-UP WITH

CHANDELIERS, LAMPS,
PENDANTS & BRACKETS.
BURNERS OF THE MOST IMPROVED CONSTRUCTION
SUPPLIED WHOLESALE AND RETAIL.

Special attention is called to our IMPROVED GLOBES for all classes of Gas Fittings. These are made with wide openings underneath to admit of an adequate supply of air, and the use of Batswing Regulator Burners, instead of ordinary Fishtails, thus giving a higher illuminating power without extra consumption of gas.

COOKING & HEATING APPARATUS OF EVERY DESCRIPTION

AGENTS FOR VERITY'S PATENT GAS FIRES.

Show Rooms:—

COMMERCIAL STREET, SHEFFIELD,

Where a large and valuable assortment of FITTINGS are constantly kept, the Shortest Notice, and upon the most reasonable CONTRACTS for a specified sum of money will be entered into before the work is commenced.

SHEFFIELD UNITED GAS LIGHT COMPANY

**Gryphon detail**

## The Gas Company Showroom

The later building of the gas showrooms, next to the old offices, have two fine carvings by the artist Philip Lindsay-Clarke. One shows a naked man rising from flames, the other a naked woman falling from the sun like Icarus with lost wings. Clarke also did carvings on the Mappin Street Institute for the Blind.

Further up Commercial Street, at the junction with Waingate, is a bank that bears a plaque stating that the building was the old stock exchange. "Sheffield Stock Exchange occupied this building between 1911-1967. The exchange was founded in 1844 at the height of the railway boom. Early trading was almost exclusively in railway stock." Later steel and colliery shares became popular.

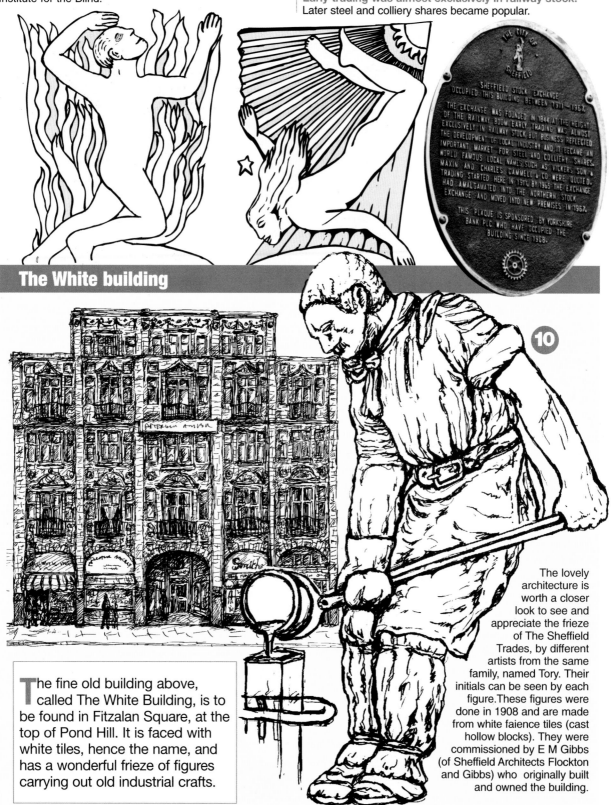

## The White building

The fine old building above, called The White Building, is to be found in Fitzalan Square, at the top of Pond Hill. It is faced with white tiles, hence the name, and has a wonderful frieze of figures carrying out old industrial crafts.

The lovely architecture is worth a closer look to see and appreciate the frieze of The Sheffield Trades, by different artists from the same family, named Tory. Their initials can be seen by each figure. These figures were done in 1908 and are made from white faience tiles (cast hollow blocks). They were commissioned by E M Gibbs (of Sheffield Architects Flockton and Gibbs) who originally built and owned the building.

**The Sheffield Trades Frieze shows the following industrial crafts:**

**1.** A silversmith (with a blowpipe) **2.** a chaser, **3.** an engineer, **4.** a file cutter, **5.** a steel roller, **6.** a cutler, **7.** a grinder (using a flat stick) **8.** a hand forger, **9.** a buffer and **10.** a steel crucible teemer (with a sweat rag in his mouth).

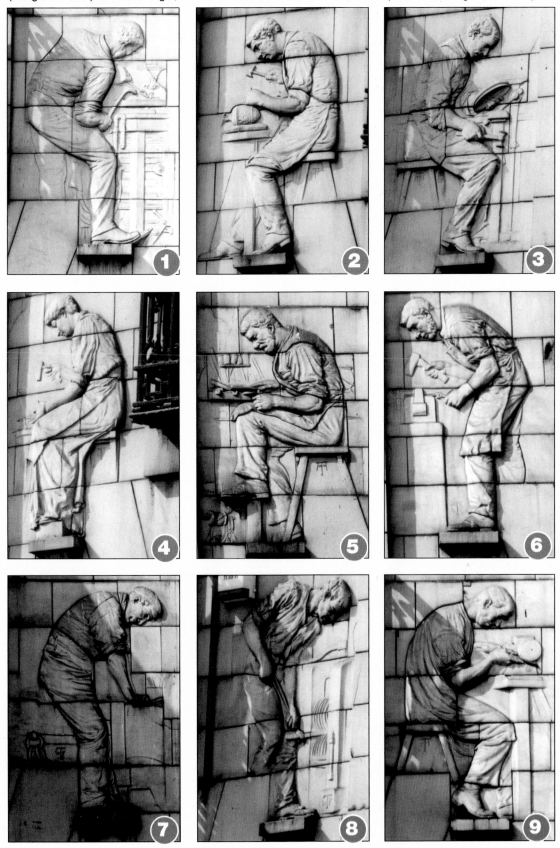

## Also in Fitzalan Square

PHOTO: STAR ARCHIVES

To the right of the White Building, on the corner with High Street, is The Marples Pub. This is a new building on the site of an older one. The Marples was a popular meeting place and full almost every night.

On December 12, 1940, in what became known as the Sheffield Blitz of World War II, this lively pub became a tomb.

In the largest single loss of life in the entire raid, a bomb scored a direct hit and claimed the lives of dozens. It was never clear how many died, but at least 60 bodies were recovered. Only 14 could be named. The rest had to be identified through belongings, such as identity cards and jewellery.

They had taken shelter in the cellars of the pub. believing themselves safe, but sadly this was not so.

**The Marples after the bomb hit. Inset: Sign today on the new building**

In the centre of Fitzalan Square is a statue of King Edward VII. This is made of bronze and was made by the sculptor Alfred Drury (1857-1944) in 1913.
The four sides of the plinth have panels on them, one bears the name Edward VII, the others show figures holding banners of the words Peacemaker, Unity and Philanthropy.

The square was built on the site of an old market.

**Right: Unity by A Drury ARA**

Statue of Edward VII

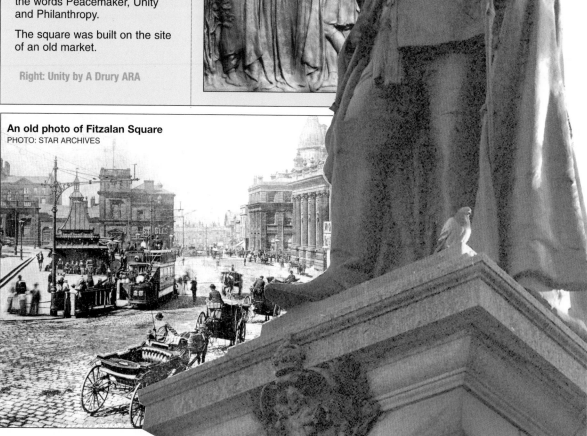

**An old photo of Fitzalan Square**
PHOTO: STAR ARCHIVES

# Crucible Steel

Just off busy Abbeydale Road, a small industrial hamlet provides a time capsule of steel production history...

A man preparing clay to use for the crucibles by 'puddling' it with his feet

**S**heffield has long held a proud reputation for knife and tool making. Even in Chaucer's time of the Middle Ages one of his Canterbury Pilgrims possessed a Sheffield blade. But it was a new type of steel production, four centuries later, that enabled the volume of steel produced to dramatically increase and expand the industry.

## The power of water

Sheffield was a perfect place to set up early industry. There were rivers to power the wheels of mills, and local resources of iron ore, wood, sandstone, lead and lime. From medieval times there had been corn mills owned by the monks of Beauchief Abbey and at Sheffield Castle, plus a mill for weapons at Kelham Island. By the late 18th century there were over 120 water powered mills lining Sheffield rivers. At Abbeydale, the Industrial Hamlet was one of the largest, powered by the River Sheaf.

The main product was scythes and earliest records of works on the site date to 1714, but the site probably goes back several centuries.

A dam collected water from the rivers to build and when the water was released the power of the flow would turn the huge wooden waterwheels of the workshops.

Waterwheel at Abbeydale

## Growth of the site

In 1777 the dam was enlarged. A field there called Sinder Hills was used to build on. This name probably dates from earlier lead smelting at the site. A tilt-hammer forge was built in 1785 and workmen's cottages in 1793, with a grinding workshop being built by 1817. Great progress was made with steel in the 18th century, with Benjamin Huntsman experimenting to produce superior quality metal (see the next pages). By the 1830's a furnace using his *crucible steel* method was installed at Abbeydale, with a pot shop for making crucibles and a furnace for melting steel. There were also other forges and warehouses, a manager's house built in 1833 and a coach house and stabling added in 1840.

## A hard place to work

The hamlet has had a battered past, with the grinding room blown up by gunpowder in 1842, in a protest against using non union labour. Twenty years later, in the same arguments, the then owner, Joshua Tyzack, was shot at five times. With fumes and grinding dust, the hamlet was a hard place to work. A boiler blew up in 1870, killing two men and in 1912 a grindstone burst, killing a scythe grinder.

Crucibles lined up in the pot shop at Abbeydale Industrial Hamlet

The crucible furnaces at the hamlet. The lids would be closed when the crucible pots had been lowered in

The Crucible Theatre is named after Huntsman's method of steel production.

## End of an era

By 1933, the hamlet had ceased production, with work moving to more up to date premises at Little London Works.

During World War II, there was a brief re-using of the place, with the furnaces being used to produce high quality steel for the war effort.

Sheffield Industrial Museums Trust (SIMT), based at Kelham Island Museum, took over the site in 1998. They have a website at **www.simt.co.uk**

**Opening times:** Abbeydale is open to the public between March and October. Monday to Thursday 10am - 4pm. Sunday 11am to 4.45pm. Open to school parties all the year round. Admission charge. Closed Fridays and Saturdays except for special events.
**Phone SIMT 0114 272 2106 for details.**

This bronze statue by artist Robin Bell stands in the lower mall at Meadowhall Shopping Precinct. It shows a man teeming crucible steel into a mould

Below, used crucibles stacked up at Abbeydale Industrial Hamlet

# Benjamin Huntsman 1704 - 1776

Huntsman was the man responsible for Sheffield becoming one of the quality steel producing centres of the world. He started his experiments around 1740. Then, Sheffield produced around 200 tons of steel a year.

A hundred years later, Sheffield produced around 20,000 tons, thanks to his new methods.

Huntsman was the third son of Quaker parents, born at Epworth in Lincolnshire on 4 June, 1704.

Little is known of his life until he was apprenticed, aged 14, to an Epworth clockmaker. Seven years later he was a clockmaker in his own right in Doncaster. There are no portraits of him, as this was against his Quaker beliefs.

Benjamin married in 1729 and had two children. Though the marriage was rocky, with his wife leaving, the couple seemed to stay on speaking terms as they were both eventually buried in the same grave at Attercliffe Chapel, in the Hill Top Cemetery.

Attercliffe Chapel at Hill Top Cemetery

In Doncaster, Huntsman was appointed to look after the town clock at Butcher Cross in 1727 and the new town clock in 1735.

As well as clockmaking, Huntsman became interested in other small engineering projects, such as locks, and also with medicine. He discovered the blister steel of the time was too crude for tools and the watch springs he wanted to make. Huntsman decided that if he could melt the raw steel in a small, heat resisting container, called a crucible, the product would be more uniform. The glassworks already operating at Catcliffe, (the kiln of which is still visible from the Parkway) used such clay pots to melt at very high temperatures, and may have helped inspire him.

Huntsman moved from Doncaster to a cottage, which is now

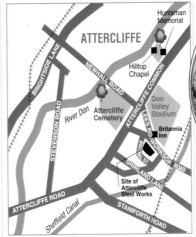

demolished, at Handsworth, then a village near Sheffield, in 1742. It is thought that here he developed his experiments on melting steel, whilst still working as a clockmaker. By 1751, however he gave up this trade and concentrated on steelmaking.

He moved to new premises he designed himself, on the Worksop Road, Attercliffe, around 1770. Shortly after, he moved again to some nearby premises later to be known as Huntsman's Row. There are other buildings also nearby that he may have used in between. The Huntsman's Row site was occupied by himself and his descendants until 1899, when the firm then moved to its final quarters at Tinsley Park Road. A building on Worksop Road, now the Britannia Inn, has the date 1772 in large, probably steel, numerals on its gable. These are said to have been made by Huntsman himself and it is generally considered that this building was Huntsman's residence for the last few years of his life.

The experiments of Huntsman were successful and brought him a great deal of work and a high reputation, but his Quaker beliefs made him not much interested in making lots of money. He did not patent his new process and there were many attempts to copy it, both in the area and further afield.

Left: The Huntsman Memorial at Hill Top Cemetery

His entirely hand-made process provided the best steel in the world for quality cutting tools and engineering parts. Steam engines needed the better quality, harder wearing steel for their components. Without this steel, the steam power input of the Industrial Revolution would have come much later.

For over a century this new method of producing cast steel was the only method of producing an ingot of steel. In the 19th century, ingots of up to 25 tons were made, casting the contents of as many as 672 crucibles into the mould over 4 hours. Later, Bessemer invented a method for a better way of bulk steel making. The crucible steel method, however, continued well into the 20th century for high quality steel making, until the electrical furnaces took over. There are now new techniques outstripping Huntsman's dreams, but he is the one that began Sheffield's longstanding reputation for high quality steel-making.

The Britannia Inn, with metal date 1772 on the gable

# Making Crucible Steel

1.Clay was pushed into a flask, which was oiled to stop clay sticking. The flask had a false bottom.

**Clay**

**Clay**

**Flask**

**False bottom on flask**

**Plug**

2.A plug was hammered into the clay filled flask with a maul, forcing the clay into the correct shape for a crucible.

3.The plug was removed and the flask lowered over a stand. The false bottom of the flask was pushed up, forcing the shaped clay out.

Shaped clay

Shaped clay forced out

Flask pushed down

Stand

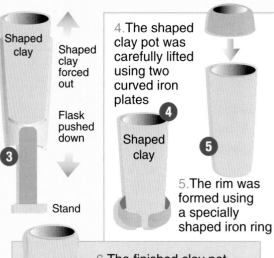

4.The shaped clay pot was carefully lifted using two curved iron plates

Shaped clay

5.The rim was formed using a specially shaped iron ring

6.The finished clay pot, or crucible was set to dry, then fired for about eight hours in an oven next to the main furnace

Charging pan

Weight of charge = around 56llbs (25kg)

7.The 'charge' (pieces of blister steel, iron and scrap, plus some charcoal) was weighed and put in the crucible. Lime was added later as a flux, fusing the impurities together and making them easier to remove

9. Lids were put on the crucibles and furnace hole lid closed. Draughts from the cellar going up the chimney got the temperature up to 1550 degrees centigrade. Melting took three to four hours.

Lid of furnace hole closed

8.The crucibles were placed in a furnace, on a fireclay stand on iron bars. Coke was packed around the crucibles. Below the iron bars a fire was lit.

Crucible lids added

1550 °C

10. The crucible full of melted steel was pulled from the furnace using long handled tongs.

The 'puller out' protected himself from the heat by wearing wet leather and sacking

The mould was held together with a ring and wedges. These were removed when the steel was set, to part the mould and remove the ingot

Mould

11.The crucible was carried to the Teeming Bay. Here the lid was removed.

Using round-headed tongs, the molten steel was poured into moulds to make ingots

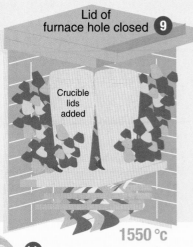

# The Queen's Tower

**Hidden away in trees, close to Norfolk Park and Supertram lines, sits a mock Tudor mini castle, built for an eccentric Victorian**

Peeping out from the treetops, the castellated towers of Queen's Tower give a tantalising glimpse of the lovely old building at present half hidden in undergrowth.

### Fanciful residence

Queen's Tower was built by a wealthy local man, Samuel Roberts between 1834 and 1837, on land owned by the 12th Duke of Norfolk. This was around the same time as the Botanical Gardens were being built and the General Cemetery too.

Roberts had an interest in Mary Queen of Scots, who had been imprisoned at the nearby Sheffield Manor. This lodge was in ruins, which upset Roberts and so he wanted to build his own new version. He commissioned Woodhead and Hirst of Doncaster to design the house for him. It was built as a mock castle in 'Tudor Gothic' style. The family crests of Samuel Roberts are still there on the building today, as are his initials, carved on the gateways, along with the Queen's Tower name.

The house was in landscaped gardens with an adjacent stable block, which included servants' quarters, a walled garden and a gate house lodge. It epitomised the Victorian idea of a romantic Tudor Manor house. The grounds were designed by Robert Marnock, who was designer and first curator of the new Botanical gardens. There were two entrances to the site, one on East Bank Road and a bigger entrance off Park Grange Road, for carriage access to the stable block. North of the mansion was a small lake with a footbridge over. Also on early maps of 1853 is what seems to be a knot garden.

Roberts even had a portion of the old Sheffield Manor lodge in his possession. It was a mullioned window, which Mary is supposed to have looked through. This was one of the main features in his new garden. Pawson and Brailsford mention the Tower in their guide book:

*"Tradition asserts that when the Queen of Scots was first taken to the Manor she nearly escaped from the window of her room. The late Mr Roberts, who was a devoted admirer of the Queen, obtained permission to remove the stonework of this mullioned window and erected it at Queen's Tower, where it is still carefully preserved."*

**Looking up at a Tudor rose on one of the gates**

Samuel Roberts never actually lived in his fairytale creation, but gave it to his son Samuel when he married. He died in 1848.

**The Main doorway**

**Queen's Tower, nestled in the undergrowth**

**Above: Painted tiles from a fireplace in the house. Note the square tile with Samuel Roberts' initials. The gold shield with lion comes from above the fireplace**

## Changes to Queen's Tower

Extensions were made to the site in 1855, with the grounds being altered and the lake removed.
During and after the Second World war the building was used by the Armed forces. They filled in some of gardens.

The biggest changes to the site came in the 1960's. A squash club was built on top of the walled garden and car parking took up some of the grounds.

The lodge was later converted into offices and the rural nature of the area was slowly swallowed up by the city.

The elegant staircase (right) was added to the building in the 1930's. The carved head below is on one of the exterior stone gateways

## Worthy of Sleeping Beauty

The Queen's Tower today is overgrown and romantically semi-ruinous. Now the greenery is trying to reclaim the whole building. One tower was demolished as it was leaning too much, and the old Manor window is lost in undergrowth, but lots of the old grandeur remains, rising from the tangles of leaves. The Tower walls are clad in ivy like some fairy tale Sleeping Beauty's enchanted castle.

Please note there is no public access to The Queen's Tower and its grounds at present.

## Plans for the future

Local businessmen Fred Meggitt and Michael Charlesworth are working on turning the site into a private residential gated village containing 90 apartments. The scheme is intended to keep the character of the old Queen's Tower and would involve redeveloping the former stables block, the house and walled gardens and adding two new blocks.

# Sir Francis Chantrey

One of the art world's most acclaimed sculptors spent his youth in Norton, Sheffield, and was eventually laid to rest there, in the lovely old churchyard

Sir Francis Legatt Chantrey, one of the most important sculptors of the early 19th century, was born in Norton, then a small village, on 7th April, 1781. He worked as a milk boy, doing early morning rounds.

## Artistic aspirations

Bust of Rev. Wilkinson in Sheffield Cathedral

After a while, Chantrey moved on to work at a general grocer's store, but didn't like the work and was much happier when he secured a job on the High Street, at a shop selling art materials. Whilst working here, in 1797, he was apprenticed to the owner Mr Ramsey to learn art skills. One of the customers, an engraver named Raphael Smith, took a liking to Chantrey and gave him drawing lessons to improve his work.

Chantrey had an inborn skill and later began to make plaster casts and carvings of the employees. His talent was noticed and he decided to try and make art his living.

He moved to 24 Paradise Square when he had finished his apprenticeship, and whilst living there he advertised in the local newspaper, then *The Iris*, asking for clients for portraits.

As his confidence grew, he moved to London, in 1802, working as a woodcarver's apprentice. He made friends with a man called Benjamin West, President of the Royal Academy, which probably helped his career.

## Fame and Fortune

By 1807 he was well known in his own right, writing to friends to tell them he was working on 8 portraits which he would sell for 20 guineas each.

In 1809 he exhibited a sculpture of The Head of Satan at the Royal Academy, which led to commissions for Greenwich Hospital. Another exhibition in 1811 brought him even more work and an enviable reputation. Marrying his cousin Ann Wale brought more wealth and he purchased several houses and a fine studio.

By 1822 he was charging around 300 guineas for a bust.

He travelled abroad, including trips to Paris and Rome and purchased marble for his works.

In 1835 he was knighted, and was a wealthy man.

## Back to his roots

1840 was his last visit to his home place of Norton. He died in November 1841. Many in London wanted him to be buried in Westminster Abbey, but he had requested his body return to the little churchyard at Norton, which it did.

The journey took six days, with the hearse and mourning car each being drawn by four horses and preceded by four men on horseback.

## The Chantrey Bequest

This fund was set up, as was his wish in his will, when his wife eventually died The money was to enable the Royal Academy to purchase British works of art for the National Collection (later the Tate Gallery).

## Lasting memorials

A local example of his work is a bust of the Rev. James Wilkinson in Sheffield Cathedral, by the North wall of the High Sanctuary. Also in Sheffield are statues of Hope and Charity, on the old Royal Infirmary on Infirmary Road, now a supermarket.

Other works include some in Westminster Abbey, and St. Paul's Cathedral in London and The Sleeping Children in Lichfield Cathedral, as well as in Manchester Town Hall, and a statue of George Washington in the state house at Boston, USA. When Chantrey died, it was decided to build

a monument of some sort. The money was raised by public subscription and in 1854 a granite obelisk was made. It was carved by Chantrey's artist friend Philip Hardwick RA.

The stone was brought from Cornwall to Hull by sea and then pulled by horses across country. The obelisk is 22 ft high, and stands on 3ft high steps. The hump of grass which it graces is all that is left of the old village green.

## St James Church, Norton

**T**his lovely old church dates from Saxon times. In front of the church is a celtic cross style war memorial. The Old Rectory, to the right of the church, is Georgian, built around 1714. The new rectory is further up the lane. First evidence of a church on this site is in 1183, when Robert Fitzranulph, who founded Beauchief Abbey, bestowed the church to this abbey.

A lot of rebuilding on an earlier church was carried out in the 13th and 14th centuries. The church was much restored in 1882, leaving it much as it looks today.

There are many fine stained glass windows, including an angel window of the 1930-40's which is a memorial to a past Reverend's wife, Annie Hall, who had lived at Norton Hall.

### The Graveyard

This is the long used last resting place for the Norton community. Many of them were in the farming or related trades. To the right side of the church is a gravestone for a scythegrinder. Nail makers lived in Norton too – there is a public house still named so.

The graveyard is no longer used for burials. They are now at Norton Cemetery on Derbyshire Lane. There is a garden of remembrance in the churchyard, however, where ashes are scattered. Now the old gravestones are lined up around the walls, as they were in a dangerously unstable state. One on the far wall opposite the church main doorway is to a Charles Hannah Glover, who was just 16 when he was *"by bloody minded men untimely slain"* in 1846. Also in the graveyard is a stone to a child of the Gillatt family, Ann, aged 4 years 5 months. It is carved with angels (right). By the side of the path to the church is the old preaching cross (bottom left), from Medieval times. It was moved to this position when the grave of Frances Chantrey was made. His grave is near the top of the path, to the left, a large slab surrounded by railings.

### Inside the church

The interior is late Norman / Early English and the tower dates from 1180 AD. The later plaster added to the inside walls has been removed to expose the original stone, warm and welcoming.

**Carvings from the font**

● **The font**

This dates from 1220 and is in the early English style. There is a salamander (above) carved on it, along with a winged head with a monk style hairdo (above, top). The salamander is thought by some to represent the devil, seen as a creature of fire, which witnesses with disgust the baptism of a child.

● **The Belfry**

This is on the left as you enter. There are eight bells altogether, which are still rung frequently.

● **The Chantrey statue**

Directly across from the porch is a statue of Chantrey. It was made after his death by sculptor J.Bell .

● **The Blythe Chapel**

This private chapel was built by the Blythe family in 1520. The Blythes lived at nearby 'Bishops House' in Meersbrook Park. Their tomb was vandalisd by troops during the civil war. There is a *piscina* in this chapel; this is where the vessels used for sevices were washed.

## Location of Norton Church

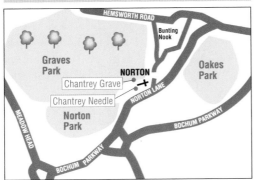

HEMSWORTH ROAD

Bunting Nook

Graves Park

NORTON

Chantrey Grave

Chantrey Needle

Norton Park

Oakes Park

NORTON LANE

BOCHUM PARKWAY

MEADOW HEAD

BOCHUM PARKWAY

## The Entrance

The main entrance to the church has a fine example of Norman zig zag carving in the arch over the door. In the porch are six carved faces on the wall. These are thought to be Norman and were found in the vaults when the church was restored in he late Nineteenth century. Along the wall of the porch is a tombstone to William Blythe of Norton Lees, who lived at Bishops House in what is now Meersbrook Park.

He was a commander during the Civil War of 1646 and was involved in ordering the destruction of Sheffield Castle. Another gravestone is that of Barbara Lee, who was buried - in an upright position - near the altar in 1670.

## Services at St James Church

**Every Sunday:**
8.00am, Holy Communion
10.30am, Sung Mass (2nd Sunday Family Worship)
6.15pm: Evensong

**Weekdays:**
Daily (except Friday)
8.00am: Morning Prayer
6.00pm: Evening Prayer

**Mass:**
6pm Tues,10am Wed, 6pm Thurs

**Telephone the rectory on (0114) 2745066 for information.**

## Bellringing

There are eight bronze bells at St. James, made in the still working bell foundry at Loughborough. The largest bell, the tenor, weighs three quarters of a ton.

The church is often looking for new bellringers. Call Geoff Vardy on (0114) 2745259. Practise nights are on Mondays, 7.30 - 9.00pm.

The old bell clapper shown left is inside the church. It is said to be from the old Beauchief Abbey and was once used as a doorstop.

**The Norman doorway of the church**

**This stone is by the path to the church**

IN MEMORY of Will^m Bailey, Scythegrinder who died June the 8th 1778 Aged 49 Years.

## Norton Hall

Next to the church is Norton Hall. This was built in 1815 by a man named Samuel Shore, though there were probably earlier buildings on the site.

The Shore family were bankers, but their bank in Church Street crashed, losing their fortune.

The hall and estate were sold in 1850, to a new owner Charles Cammell.

He added further features and rooms, including a dining room and a billiards room.

It is now private apartments. The old grounds of the hall became Graves Park.

# Do you know where they are?

See if you can spot these carvings when you next walk around Sheffield City Centre and vicinity

**1. A bat winged beast from George Street (off High Street)**

**2.** An old fire insurance symbol of a sun, from the Division Street Fire station.

**3. Coat of arms, also from the Division Street Fire station.**

**4.** A roundel from the Central Library main entrance. It shows a telescope, stars, clouds, sun and moon. Other carvings at the door show disciplines such as science and literature.

**5. Lion from Castle Square in the City Centre.** A copy of one of four which stood on the old Crimea Monument, once near the town hall. These four new lions, on brick pillars, are by artist Chris Boulton. He restored the best preserved originals and cast the new winged beasts in 1991.

**6.** This Greyhound is from the long closed pub of the same name, at Gibraltar Street's junction with Copper Street. It is on a stone lintel over the corner door of what is now a shop.

**7. This kangaroo is over the doorway at 44 Wellington Street, near the present fire station. It is an old trademark of Sorby Roberts & Son, who made knives, etc.**

**8.** This Pointer dog is on Bailey Lane, off Trippet Lane. It is the trademark of an old firm that used to occupy the building.

**9.** A crowned head from a plaque on what is now a bank - at the corner of Pinstone Street and Charles Street

70

# The Wicker

A well known landmark in the city are the arches that span gracefully over the busy thoroughfare of The Wicker...

The Wicker Arches were opened in 1849, as part of the new viaduct built to carry the new Manchester, Sheffield and Lincolnshire Railway over the Don Valley.

## The name

The name 'Wicker' has a few possible origins that people have toyed with. One is from the wic or bend in the river (Don). Another is that it is from the old word wick, meaning near, as in near the old Sheffield Castle. It could also be from the old Norse word, vikir, which means willow, that probably once grew in the marshy area near the river. The willow would have been collected to make into wicker baskets. Also popular is the idea that the name comes from the wicker targets that archers used to practice on in the area, which used to be the Assembly Green of the castle. All kinds of sports and games would probably have been held here.

## Building the arches

The Wicker arches were designed by Sheffield born engineer William Fowler, who was also later responsible for building the Forth Railway Bridge.

The arches were begun mid 1930's by Blackie and Shortridge, the same time as Victoria Station was being built.

John Shortridge, also responsible for the construction of The Wicker Arches is buried in Christ Church, Heeley, Sheffield. The obelisk marking his grave is just inside the churchyard gates, on the left. It stands on a huge granite base.

The central arch of the Wicker Arches is over 70ft long. The stone came from a quarry at Wharncliffe Crags.

On the arches are four crests carved in stone. These represent the MS&L Railway Company, The Duke of Norfolk, The Earl of Yarborough and The Sheffield Town trustees.

During the Sheffield Flood of 1864, debris piled up against the Wicker arches, backlogging water which then overspilled into the Wicker. Water came up to the Lodge Public House, on Spital Hill, now a derelict motorcycle shop. The name Spital Hill comes from the fact that an old Hospital used to stand there.

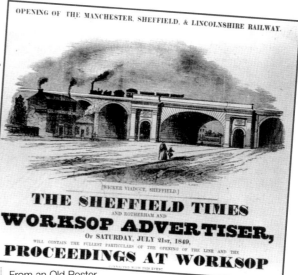

OPENING OF THE MANCHESTER, SHEFFIELD, & LINCOLNSHIRE RAILWAY.

[WICKER VIADUCT, SHEFFIELD.]

**THE SHEFFIELD TIMES**
AND ROTHERHAM AND
**WORKSOP ADVERTISER,**
OF SATURDAY, JULY 21st, 1849,
WILL CONTAIN THE FULLEST PARTICULARS OF THE OPENING OF THE LINE AND THE
**PROCEEDINGS AT WORKSOP**

From an Old Poster

During the Sheffield Blitz in World War II, the arches were damaged by a bomb. Many people will still remember walking though the Wicker after the Blitz and seeing the flames and destruction, including a tram split in half lying across the road.

In later years the arches were partly demolished during the electrification of the line.

In 1990, the arches were restored to their former appearance as part of the regeneration of the Don Valley.

A plaque under the arches telling their history was unveiled by Hugh Sykes the Master Cutler and Chairman of Sheffield Development Corporation on 22 April 1991.

PHOTO: THE STAR ARCHIVES

This was the scene in The Wicker on December 13, the day after the first Blitz on the city.

Below: an old scene in The Wicker, with the arches in the background as a tram trundles past.

The Wicker in 1996

PHOTO: THE STAR ARCHIVES

## Victoria Station

At the East side of the arches there used to be a lift up to the old Victoria Station platform. The station is now gone, but the old railway hotel, The Victoria, is still there. The old Victoria station was accessed either by the lift, for a small fee, or a flight of stone steps. The other way was from Blonk Street, up the ramp called Victoria Station Road, though known as Victoria Station Approach by most people.

When the station opened in September 1851. It was described in Pawson and Brailsford's Guide to Sheffield as

*"A handsome structure near the cattle market,"* ....
*"one of the finest and most complete in the kingdom."*

Above, an old print of the Victoria Hotel and right, an advertisement marking a royal visit to the station

## The war memorial

Under the left hand arch is a memorial to the memory of the Great Central Railwaymen who gave their lives in the Great War (1914-18).

There are over 1,300 names on the plaque, which is around 21ft by 6ft. it was placed there around 1920.

It is hoped that the memorial can be moved in the near future to a spot where it is less open to graffiti and vandalism, perhaps by the Victoria Station Hotel..

This Stag beetle is carved on the left of the door of the old Station Hotel near the Wicker Arches. It nestles in oak leaves and acorns. On the other side of the door is carved a frog.

## Lady's Bridge

This old bridge is the way into the Wicker from the City Centre. It is the first established crossing over the River Don. This crossing was near the old Sheffield Castle, so an important and busy area area. It was so named because an old chapel stood on the bridge.

The bridge of 1485 was widened three times, in 1761, 1864 and 1909, to cope with the increasing number of people. Some of the 1485 structure still forms the bridge there today.

### WICKER WEIR

This was first mentioned in 1581 but could be even older. There were two water wheels run here. One was for the Wicker Tilt, run by Benjamin Blonk, who later gave his name to Blonk Street.

The other was the Wicker Wheel, which was around where the SADACCA building is now.

an old poster

The Exchange Brewery was founded at Lady's Bridge in 1852. The golden cornsheaf and hops over the entrance archway still shine bright, though it is no longer the Exchange Brewery.

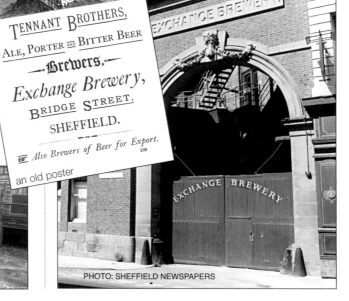

PHOTO: SHEFFIELD NEWSPAPERS

## The SADACCA Building

This ornate old building, on the right hand side of the Wicker walking down from the Castlegate direction, has a splendid facade with interesting carvings.

It was once the Clyde Steel and Iron Works, owned by a local man called Samuel Osborn, who was born in 1826.

Osborn was a successful industrialist, and became Master Cutler in 1873 and Mayor of Sheffield in 1891.

His firm became the sole maker of a special kind of steel called Mushet's, which cut through harder metals than other steels and so was ideal for making into drills etc.

This steel was developed by a man called Robert Mushet, (1811-1891) who was from The Forest of Dean.

Mushet had discovered that adding tungsten to the crucible melt when making steel made the resulting steel much harder and also made it harden better in the open air.

He called it his "self hardening steel' but it soon became known as 'Robert Mushet Special Steel' (RMS). It was the first real tool steel

Mushet made a deal with the Titanic Steel Company in Gloucestershire, but when they closed down in 1870 he made a deal with Samuel Osborn. This deal gave Osborn a virtual monopoly on tool quality steel. Mushet's two sons moved to Sheffield to oversee the making of RMS.

Some of the carvings from the front of the building

The old firm has been renovated and is now used by SADACCA (Sheffield and District Afro Caribbean Community Association).

## The Lion Cafe

The Riverside Court Hotel in the Wicker used to be the Lyons Cafe and shops during the 50's. The old name can still be seen, inlaid with mosaic tiles on the floor in the entrance porch.

Also worth a look, just off the Wicker on Stanley Street, is a classic 1930 design building called Stanley House.

## Colourful tiles

Next to the river near Lady's Bridge are a group of attractive castellated style buildings with lovely mixed brown brickwork, which have in recent years being cleaned up beautifully.

According to the informative council board near the site these buildings, called Castle House, are in the so called 'Flemish Style' with elaborate glazed bricks. They were built in 1900 by John Henry Bryars.

Bryars was a vet who looked after the horses used by the nearby Midlands Railway Company at Victoria Station.

The horses were stabled in Castle House, which also had a farrier's shop and sick room.

The horses stabling is still there in the yards at the back of the building.

On the river side wall of the building is a stone plaque bearing symbols of the animals and veterinary practice, an echo of the use it was once put to. The name J H Bryars can still be made out too, but is almost worn away. There is a side doorway that used to lead down to a dog shelter. The words 'dog's home' are still just visible.

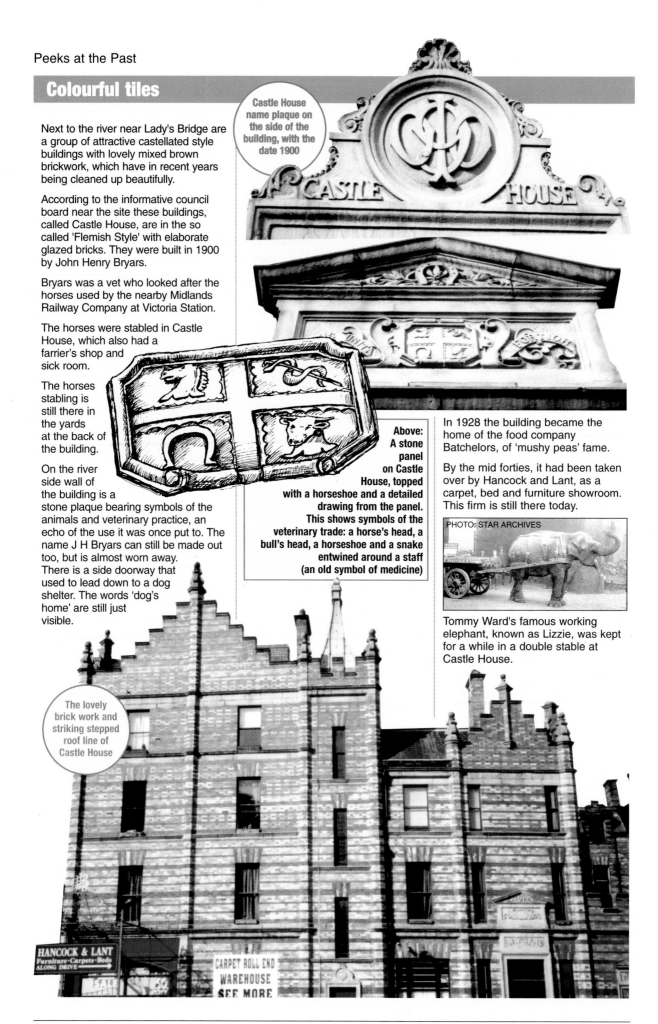

Castle House name plaque on the side of the building, with the date 1900

**Above: A stone panel on Castle House, topped with a horseshoe and a detailed drawing from the panel. This shows symbols of the veterinary trade: a horse's head, a bull's head, a horseshoe and a snake entwined around a staff (an old symbol of medicine)**

In 1928 the building became the home of the food company Batchelors, of 'mushy peas' fame.

By the mid forties, it had been taken over by Hancock and Lant, as a carpet, bed and furniture showroom. This firm is still there today.

PHOTO: STAR ARCHIVES

Tommy Ward's famous working elephant, known as Lizzie, was kept for a while in a double stable at Castle House.

The lovely brick work and striking stepped roof line of Castle House

HANCOCK & LANT
Furniture·Carpets·Beds
ALONG DRIVE

SALE 50

CARPET ROLL END
WAREHOUSE
SEE MORE

# Birley Spa

Gable end of
the bath house

*One of Sheffield's hidden places is an old spa bath house, once bustling with people 'taking the waters' or listening to the strains of a band playing on the balcony..*

Birley Spa at Hackenthorpe was where a bath house was built in 1843. The water still flows there from a natural spring which has never dried out in living memory. Pools offered visitors the chance to sample the healing waters at various temperatures. These lovely old baths have now been given a facelift.

## A trendy place to be

The word Birley comes from the old English words *BURH*, meaning a fortified area, and *LEY*, meaning a clearing or cleared ground. It is likely there was indeed a fort here, as it is close to the old boundary between the old kingdoms of Mercia and Northumbria, as well as the old Roman Road called Ryknield Street. The area, however, had been in use long before, even as far back as the Mesolithic period (3000 - 8000 years ago). In 1951 flints (right) from that period were found close by.

**Flints, not to scale**

The baths were commissioned there in 1843 by Earl Manvers of Thoresby Hall. Local people often refer to the spot as the Roman Baths, though there is no evidence to support this, except word of mouth. It is possible the Romans had a bath house here, close to their old road and fort.

There were indeed earlier buildings on the site than Earl Manvers buildings. A stone structure dated 1701 used to stand there and old records mention a man called George Hancock paying for a building there in 1789.

The Earl Manvers development of the spa was an ambitious one. Two bridges were to cross the stream that flows through the deep wooded valley, and several grottos and walks were planned, though no one knows if these features ever made it to reality from the drawing board.

What was built then, the combined hotel and bath house in the Dutch style of architecture, is what is left today. The building has a single storey hotel, with the baths underneath. Water temperature is a constant 53°F (11.6°C)

An advert for staff appeared on March 25th 1843, in the Sheffield & Rotherham Independent (see below) and a man called George Eadon and his wife were selected. The place was then called the Bath Hotel and the wages were £20 per year, plus free rent and coal.

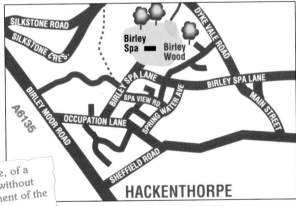

HACKENTHORPE

## The tariff

There were different baths, with different costs, to be taken at the spa. The best marble hot bath cost 2/6 (two shillings and sixpence - about 12.5p), an ordinary hot bath cost 1/6 (7.5p), a tepid bath 1/- (5p), a large cold bath sixpence (2.5p), a ladies cold bath ninepence (less than 4p) and a hot and cold shower bath also ninepence. No bathing was allowed on a Sunday, unless by medical recommendation. Annual subscribers could recommend a 'poor person' to be allowed to have a bathe. An omnibus ran from the Commercial Inn in Sheffield to take people there. The rich and poorer alike favoured the medicinal dips, and in May 1843, the Duke of Portland came from Welbeck and stayed for a week, taking hot baths daily.

WANTED a man and his wife, of a good Moral Characters and without family, to take the Management of the BATHS at Birley Spa...

The pond at Birley Spa

## Failing numbers

Popular as they were, the baths did not manage to make a profit and by 1895 only one plunge bath remained. The hotel ceased to function as such about 1878. Changes in bathing prices and seven different proprietors between 1843 and 1012 still didn't do the trick and in 1912 plans were made to sell the baths by auction, along with two nearby cottages.

## A new lease of life

George Moulson, from Handsworth - Woodhouse bought the site, for £930 and developed it during the 1920s and 30s. He and partner, William Smith, are the ones that turned Birley Spa into the pleasure ground that many older residents of the area remember so fondly. They added a wishing well, a sandpit, a paddling pool, a boating lake (the large pond that is still there today) and a 'wonder tree'. This tree was an ancient oak, and it was so gnarled it was a favourite pastime to imagine animals and faces within its shapes. There were also wooden horse rides like the one shown above. This time was a high spot in the life of the spa and it was described in publicity leaflets as 'The Children's paradise".

Sunday School outings to the spot were popular, and picnics. Bands would play music on the balcony of the baths building and parties from the surrounding villages came.

## Moving on

When the second World War broke out, the Spa was closed, as government policy was to stop large crowds gathering together. A few years before, tennis courts had been laid out just above the ground to the west of Rose Cottages, which are part of the site. A pavilion for players was also erected.

As well as the Rose Cottages in the Spa grounds prior to WW2 were two bungalows and a caravan. All these tenants obtained water from a pump.

## Last days

When the war was over, Mr Smith sold the site to Sanderson Bros. and Newbold. They owned it a short while before selling it to Sheffield Corporation in the 1950's. The Spa buildings were still lit by paraffin lamps, until 1955. Just after this, the once thriving bath was left to a sad fate of neglect.

*The restored bath house building at Birley Spa today*

## Saved from the brink

In the 1960's, when research showed that in fact the baths were not Roman, but Victorian, it was decided by the council that the buildings, in a sorry state of decay, should be demolished. A local architect got involved, resulting in the building being listed and so it was saved.

The idea of a Community Centre in the house, for the people of Hackenthorpe, extended its life, though the outside balcony had to be demolished for safety. The nearby Rose Cottages were also demolished and replaced by two new houses given the same name.

Over the following years nothing much was done to preserve the building, though in 1986, £6,000 was spent repairing chimney stacks and roof and repainting the exterior and interior.

## Beginning the clear up

In 1989, a group of people met in the Normanton Springs Inn. This meeting resulted in the Shirebrook Conservation Group being formed, with 12 members. In co-operation with the Countryside Management Unit and with help from local schools, they restored much of Birley Spa and the surrounding area. The bath was cleaned out and repaired, with police frogmen helping clean out the large amount of debris thrown in by vandals. Electric lighting was reinstated and several thousand wildlife attractive trees and shrubs were planted. Seats and wooden fences were erected and paths were upgraded.

## The Spa bath house today

In December 1998, successful grant applications to the Heritage Lottery Fund and South Yorkshire Forest Environment Trust meant that a full restoration of the Community Hall and Bath House could be carried out.

The building was reopened in July 2002, with support and co-operation from Sheffield City Council's Countryside Planning Service, Sheffield Countryside Conservation Trust, local schools and police. It is now part of the Shire Brook Valley Local Nature Reserve. Railings (shown above) at the top of the drive down to the spa show Lord Manvers coat of arms, with latin motto 'pie repone te' which means rest with confidence in God. They also show some of the wildlife to be seen around Birley Spa.

■ The Community Hall can be booked from the Housing Office by telephoning (0114) 2039208/9 ■ The Bath House is open to the public by prior appointment. Admission free. Contact Shire Brook Conservation Group on (0114) 2692528 for details.

# James Montgomery

*Originally from Irvine in Ayrshire, Scotland, newspaper editor, poet and hymn writer James Montgomery had a major impact on his adopted home of Sheffield.*

James Montgomery was born in Scotland in 1771, the eldest son of Irish parents. When he was four, he returned to Ireland with his mother. His father went to be a missionary in Barbados. Both his parents died whilst carrying out missionary work.

### Early Years

James Montgomery came from a religious family. His parents belonged to the Moravian Brethren and were heavily involved in missionary work. They sent their son James to school in Leeds and in 1783 they went to the West Indies to carry on their missionary work. But their devotion to the cause cost them their lives. In 1790 his mother died of a fever and a year later his father died too. Later Montgomery wrote a poem expressing his loss:

*"Sweet seas and smiling shores!*
*Where no tornado demon roars;*
*Resembling that celestial clime. Where with the spirits of the Blest, From all their toils my parents rest."*

James Montgomery stayed at the Leeds school until he was 16, and it was thought that he would then enter the ministry like his parents. But either he had no vocation or couldn't afford the fees - he went into business instead. He had a spell of working in a shop in Wakefield, then in Wath, near Rotherham, but grew tired of this quickly.

He was passionate about poetry and in 1789 went to London in an attempt to get his poems published, but this failed and he journeyed back to Wath for a while. His love life didn't fare much better than his poetry at this time, for he fell in love with a woman called Hannah, but she married another, at least giving him some poetical inspiration about lost love.

### Montgomery the editor

Montgomery moved to Sheffield in 1792, as assistant to a Mr Joseph Gale, the editor and owner of the radical Sheffield Register. This newspaper was on virtually the same site as The Star and Telegraph stands today, at Hartshead. It was a weekly publication just four pages long, measuring 19 x 12 inches, and had a circulation of around 2,000. As well as being a newspaper the business had a shop and publishing office.

It was as a clerk that Montgomery was employed, but just two years later Gale fled to America after upsetting the authorities with his outspoken views and Montgomery took over the newspaper, helping out Mr Gales' two sisters who worked there. He later changed the name to the Sheffield Iris and the first edition of this new publication was printed on Friday July 4, 1794. The editions were the same size as The Iris and cost fourpence (about 2p)

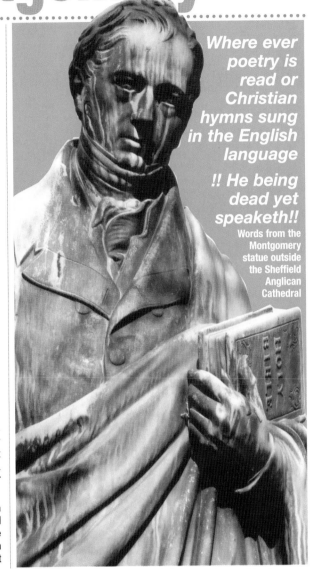

*Where ever poetry is read or Christian hymns sung in the English language*

*!! He being dead yet speaketh!!*

Words from the Montgomery statue outside the Sheffield Anglican Cathedral

It listed the publisher as James Montgomery and Co. The 'Co.' being Reverend Benjamin Naylor, a minister at the Upper Chapel on Norfolk Street. Montgomery later bought him out and ran the paper himself.

Montgomery lived above the newspaper printing shop at Hartshead and would have been there throughout the cholera epidemic that swept through the city in 1832.

In 1834, Montgomery laid the foundation stone for the Cholera Monument which was later built to commemorate the dead.

Left: The old Iris office at Hartshead. Below: A mast head from The Iris of 1820

The Iris;
THE SHEFFIELD ADVERTISER

He was as outspoken as his forerunner and ended up in trouble and even prison, on a number of occasions. He became known as a champion of the less fortunate members of society.

One of the instances which landed him in hot water in 1795 was his critical newspaper article about a disturbance in the city including the killing of two citizens and the wounding of several more. He spoke out against the event and the colonel who had let military volunteers carry out the shooting. Montgomery ended up with a six month spell in York Castle jail for his actions, as well as a £30 fine. Earlier he had been fined £20 and jailed for 3 months after printing a ballad about the French capture of the Bastille.

According to Pawson and Brailsford's 1879 guide to Sheffield. Montgomery is said to have stated in The Iris:

*"A person, who shall be nameless, plunged with his horse among the unarmed, defenceless people and wounded with his sword men, women and children."*

Another of his campaigns was to stop children being used as chimney sweeps and he was actively against slavery.

While Montgomery was in jail, he penned a poem about his experience:

## PRISON AMUSEMENTS

### Written in York Castle 14 June 1796

*In this sweet place, where freedom reigns,*
*Secured by bolts and snug in chains;*
*Where innocence and guilt together*
*Roost like two turtles of a feather;*
*Where debtors safe at anchor lie*
*From saucy duns and bailiffs sly;*
*Where highwaymen and robbers stout*
*Would, rather than break in, break out;*
*Where all's so guarded and recluse,*
*That non his liberty can lose;*
*Here each may, as his means afford,*
*Dine like a pauper or a lord,*
*And those who can't the cost defray*
*My live to dine another day.*

Montgomery sold The Iris in 1825, to a Mr John Blackwell, a printer and bookseller on Norfolk Row. The last edition, in September, had a farewell letter to the readers from Montgomery.

## Montgomery the poet and hymn writer

As well as running the Sheffield Iris, Montgomery was also a prolific writer of poetry. The lack of earlier success in London had not deterred him. Later, when the newspaper was doing well, it gave him the time and income to be able to indulge his passion.

He printed his poems at the Iris offices. One of his first publications, "The Wanderer of Switzerland", in 1806, had bad reviews, but to the reviewer's annoyance the adverse publicity had the opposite effect:

*"We believe it is scarcely possible to sell three editions of a work absolutely without merit."*
(Edinburgh Review, January 1807)

But many people appreciated Montgomery's works. His poem "The World Before The Flood" was well received and the poet Ebeneezer Elliott dedicated a poem called "Spirits and Men" to him.

Montgomery also composed hundreds of hymns. Many are still in use today, with Angels From The Realms of Glory probably being the most famous.

His other hymns include: According To Thy Gracious Word, Bright and Joyful Is The Morn, Go to Dark Gethsemane and How Beautiful Is The Sight.

## Last Days

James Montgomery lived at Hartshead until 1836, then, along with the two Gales sisters, he moved to a better environment and grander premises at The Mount, Broomhill.

### The Mount

This impressive mansion, on Glossop Road in Broomhill, comprised of eight dwellings built for the more affluent, and was designed by an architect called William Flockton in the 1830's. James Montgomery lived at number 4 until his death in 1854. The building is now privately owned by an insurance company.

The old Hartshead premises were eventually pulled down to make room for extensions of the later newspaper, The Sheffield Telegraph, now still The Star and Telegraph newspaper offices at York Street.

## The Montgomery Medal

In 1851, Sheffield School of Design was given some funding to produce a silver "Montgomery Medal". This was to be given to artists as an award for excellence. The first one to earn one was a sculptor called Charles Green.

Below: The Mount, Montgomery's old home

# The monument

When James Montgomery died, in his sleep, in 1854, there was a public funeral at the the General Cemetery, on Cemetery Road. A monument to him was erected on his grave. The statue, which was bought from money raised by public subscription, was designed by an artist named John Bell and cast at Coalbrookdale around 1860.

This statue was later moved from the General Cemetery to it's place today, at the side of the Sheffield Anglican Cathedral. It shows Montgomery holding a copy of the bible.

On the monument is written

*James Montgomery, born at Irvine, Scotland, Nov 4th 1771; died at the Mount, Sheffield (after a residence in the town of 62 years). April 30th, 1854, in the 84th year of his age. The teachers, scholars and friends of Sunday Schools in Sheffield, assisted by public subscription, have erected this monument in memory of their revered townsman. ... "Here lies interred beloved by all who knew him, the Christian poet patriot and philanthropist. Where ever poetry is read or Christian hymns are sung in the English language !! He being dead yet speaketh!!"*

There are also extracts from two of his poems, The Grave and Prayer.

**The Montgomery Theatre**

Right:
The statue in place at the General Cemetery

This window, in the High Sanctuary of Sheffield Anglican Cathedral, was given in 1880 by J.N Mappin in memory of James Montgomery. It is the work of W.E Dixon of London and Sheffield and replaces an earlier window of 1857, also from Mappin in memory of Montgomery.

A fountain on Broad Lane (right) was later erected in Montgomery's memory. The inscription is well worn now, but his name can just be made out at the bottom. It was later converted to a street lamp.

The Montgomery Theatre on Surrey Street was also named after him, as well as some streets in the city.

On the side of the present Star and Telegraph buildings, on the Hartshead side and about halfway up the wall, a plaque records the earlier publication brought to life here

HERE STOOD THE OFFICE OF
SHEFFIELD IRIS
SHEFFIELD'S FIRST NEWSPAPER
1787 ~ 1874
THIS TABLET COMMEMORATES
ITS FAMOUS EDITOR
JAMES MONTGOMERY
POET & HYMN WRITER

The plaque commemorating The Iris, from the wall of the present newspaper building, which is on the same site at York Street and Hartshead

These winged animals can be found on the cathedral walls, to the left of where the Montgomery statue stands

## Gargoyles, lions and poets

On the right hand side of the Montgomery memorial are a most impressive set of buildings. The most ornate is Parade Chambers.

This Tudor style, red brick riot of carvings is on the corner of High Street and East Parade.

It was designed by architect M E Hadfield in 1883. Pawson and Brailsford, a stationery and printing firm, occupied the building. The 'Illustrated guide to Sheffield', often quoted in this book, is an excellent example of their workmanship and shows why they had a good reputation.

The style of decoration, with gargoyles and grotesques, is a reflection of its position next to the old parish church, (now cathedral). Henry Pawson of the company also used to be a churchwarden.

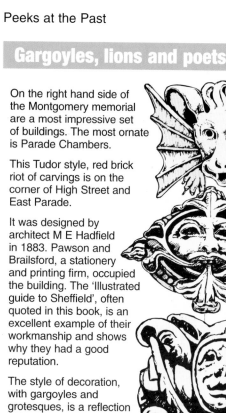

Other carvings are those of Chaucer, author of The Canterbury Tales and Caxton (inventor of the printing press). They can be recognised by their initials carved beneath them.

Initials of the company, P & B, can also be seen on the building, as well as the date 1883, when the building was constructed.

Heads of Geoffrey Chaucer and William Caxton

A green man type lion from Parade Chambers, in the Pawson and Brailsford Building

PHOTO: STAR ARCHIVES

## Coles Corner

Opposite the ornate building above is what used to be a favourite meeting spot for Sheffielders.

"Coles Corner", now a bank, was the old site of the Cole Brothers store which later moved to a site opposite the City Hall, at Barker's Pool. This store changed its name to John Lewis Partnership in 2002. The old store was a well known establishment in the city and is described in Pawson and Brailsford's guide to Sheffield:

"Sheffield will possess central streets rivalling in width and in the beauty of their architecture those of the best towns in the provinces. As a specimen of this class of buildings we give an illustration of the large establishment of Messrs. Cole Brothers, which occupies a large commanding position opposite the Parish Church. The building, which is being greatly enlarged, is an irregular square, having a frontage of 86 feet to Church Street, 94 feet to Fargate and a corner frontage of 20 feet, in which is a main entrance, towards High Street. It is built in the Modern French style of architecture and has five storeys."

# The Cutlers' Hall

The Sheffield Cutlers' Hall as it looks today

Date stone from the first hall

**Opposite the Anglican Cathedral stands the Cutlers' Hall. This building is the proud meeting place of 'The Company of Cutlers in Hallamshire in the County of York'.**

Sheffield is a name that has long been associated with cutlery, even as far back as the 14th century. The poet chaucer, in his Canterbury Tales, wrote of the Miller in his Reeves tale carrying a "Sheffield thwitel (knife) in his hose."

## The formation of the Company of Cutlers

The world 'cutlery' itself is thought to come from the old Latin word CULTELLUS - meaning a knife and also the old French word COUTELIER, any item with a cutting edge. In fact cutlery includes anything that will cut, eg. knives, scissors, razors, scythes etc. Forks and spoons are really called 'flatware'.

In early times the cutlery makers, apprenticeship and standards were controlled by the Manor Court. To keep a track of who was making what, trade marks were developed, the first being given to a man by the name of William Elles in 1554. The industry was developing fast and became too much for the Court to administrate, as well as their other duties, so a special Cutlers' Jury was begun to do the job. This was the first step. The Jury was made a more formal body, with Royal approval, on 23rd April 1624 and The Company of Cutlers was born.

The company was to control trademarks, apprenticeships, hours, punishment of offenders and quality of cutlery items.

## Members of the Company

- **The Master Cutler:** Holds office for one year. He can nominate an honorary **Mistress Cutler**, usually his wife, or occasionally his daughter.
- **The Senior Warden.**
- **The Junior Warden.**
- Six 'Searchers' who originally had the right to enter property and search out badly or illegally made goods.
- **24 Assistants**

Any other members are known as the Commonality or Freeman. Originally they would have been makers who had served an apprenticeship of at least seven years, which was recorded by the Company. By the mid 18th century there were often over 300 boys apprenticed every year. After this, if over 21, they would apply to the Company to be given their own trade mark, or Freedom. They could then work as a cutler. Many trade marks are symbols or one letter, which made it easier for earlier times when many could not read or write. Now they are Directors of companies who make cutlery, edge tools etc within the boundaries of Hallamshire.

The Cutlers' emblem outside on the hall roofline

## ABOUT THE HALLS

### The First Cutlers' Hall: 1638-1725

After the formation of the Company of Cutlers, they needed a place to use as a headquarters. They had been meeting in an inn at Fargate, opposite Norfolk Row, but wanted their own place. The first of the three halls built over the years, all on the same site as today, was in 1638. The land was bought for £69 and 12 shillings. (a shilling is around 5p of today's money). There are no details of this hall surviving.

### The Second Cutlers' Hall: 1725-1832

The first hall was demolished in May 1725 and a new one put in its place, at a cost of £430 and 10 shillings.

But by 1776, it was thought that a bigger and better hall was needed. At first the Cutlers looked for a new site to build on, but after casting around and finding this idea too costly, they decided to stay where they were. A plaque that was over the door of this building is still to be found in the present hall.

### The Third Cutlers' Hall: 1832- present

By 1827, the second hall was in a sorry state and so it was decided to demolish it. Designs from two architects, Samuel Worth and Benjamin Broomhead Taylor, were both used as no one could choose between the two plans.

The foundation stone was laid in 1832, by the then Master Cutler John Blake. Six weeks later, aged only 49, he died in a cholera epidemic which swept the city. This third hall cost around £9,000, with a further thousand or so spent on furnishings.

In 1867 the hall was extended with the addition of the Large Banqueting Hall and the Hadfield Hall and in 1881 the frontage was extended to give it the appearance we see today. It is now a Grade II listed building. The stainless steel doors were added in 1964.

### The Emblem

The Company of Cutlers' emblem includes crossed swords, (for the Cutlers), a green 'field' with sheaves of corn and crossed arrows (Sheffield was originally called Sheafield and the arrows are from the Heraldic emblem for the City), a helmet and an elephant. The elephant represents the ivory, which was used to make the handles of cutlery. In fact in the hall itself are more than 456 elephants in one form or another. The motto reads:

*"Pour y Parvenir a Bonne Foi"*

roughly translated as "for the attaining of good faith." The ones on the outside of the hall are the first form of emblem, granted in 1638, without the Sheffield heraldic addition.

This is a building which some believe is the first hall, but others think it is the inn which stood in Fargate

### Inside the Cutlers' Hall

■ **The Foyer:** From here is the sweeping staircase up to the other rooms. In the floor is a mosaic version of the above emblem, the later version granted in 1875. On show in a case are the first stainless steel knives to be made, in 1914, by Harry Brearley, who worked for Thomas Firth and Sons and discovered this new form of steel in 1913. They have xylonite, an early form of plastic as handles, instead of ivory. A pair of scissors made for the Great Exhibition of 1851 is in a case opposite. A more recent Millennium Sword is also on display.

Also on the walls are two stone tablets, one from the first hall of 1638 and one, above a fireplace and dated 1692. This was found at West Bar, in a house that belonged to a Mr Tobias Ellis, Master Cutler in 1718. It was moved here in 1912. Nearby is a wooden board, decorated with the 1638 Cutlers' emblem, the oldest painting in the building. The elephant looks very odd, but the artist had probably never seen one!.

■ **The Reception Room:**
In this grand room there are often Civil weddings taking place. On the walls are very large, ornate gilt mirrors, bought in 1954 for £50 each.

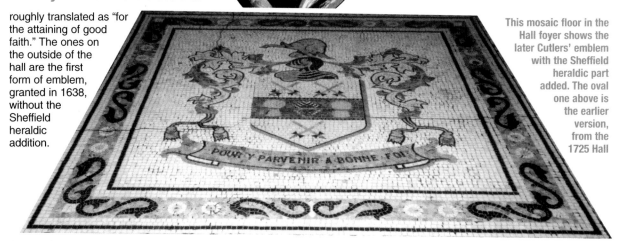

This mosaic floor in the Hall foyer shows the later Cutlers' emblem with the Sheffield heraldic part added. The oval one above is the earlier version, from the 1725 Hall

The chandelier in the Silver Vestibule, from the SS Olympic

The Norfolk Knife (below) and advert for the firm that made it from the 1879 Illustrated Guide to Sheffield by Pawson and Brailsford (left).

JOSEPH RODGERS & SONS
LIMITED.

CUTLERS

By Special Appointment to Her Majesty.

6, NORFOLK ST., SHEFFIELD,
AND
No. 4, CULLUM STREET, FENCHURCH STREET,
LONDON, E.C.,

MERCHANTS, AND MANUFACTURERS OF

CUTLERY OF EVERY DESCRIPTION,

*Silver and Plated Desserts, &c.*

DEALERS IN SILVER,
BEST SHEFFIELD AND ELECTRO-PLATED WARES,
AND MOST OTHER ARTICLES OF SHEFFIELD MANUFACTURE.

The demand for J. R. and Sons' productions having considerably increased, they have, in order to meet it, greatly extended their Manufacturing Premises and Steam Power; and, for the convenience of Merchants and the Trade, they keep a large Stock of Cutlery at their London Establishment. They beg to caution the Public against spurious goods, offered by unprincipled houses, bearing their name and made to imitate their genuine Manufactures. A considerable quantity has been recently seized in the Port of London, and condemned by the Officers of Her Majesty's Customs.
To distinguish Articles of Joseph Rodgers and Sons' Manufacture, be careful to notice that they bear their Corporate Mark—thus

(CORPORATE ✳ ⊠ MARK.)

■ **The Drawing Room:**
This is where many grand meals are eaten. On the walls are Banners from the battle of Waterloo and a portrait of the Duke of Edinburgh. This is only partly in colour, as the artist died before finishing it. Another portrait shows the 'Old Man of Dore', an early cutler called George Wainwright who is said to still hang around the place as the resident ghost. The doors have ornate handle plates depicting gryphons.

■ **The Silver Vestibule:** Here are glass cases with many fine examples of silver, still used on special occasions. Also there is a portrait of the sculptor Francis Leggatt Chantrey RA (1781-1841) and an example of his work in the form of a bust of Sir Walter Scott.

A stone over the fireplace has the date 1708, with the cutlers emblem and was found in Coal Pit Lane, (now Cambridge Street). From the ceiling hangs an ornate glass light fitting. This is from the sister ship to the ill fated Titanic, the SS Olympic, which was broken up in 1936 .

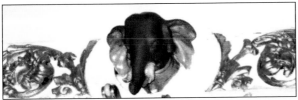

One of the many elephants dotted around the hall. This one is over a door frame into the Banqueting Hall

■ **The Banqueting Hall:** The main banquet and ball room when the present 1832 hall was built. It is used for many events, including dinner dances and every October, the installation of the new Master Cutler for that year.
An impressive dome graces the ceiling, decorated with the Cutlers' motto and significant dates in their history. A full length portrait of Thomas Jessop, who founded the city's hospital for women, and was Master Cutler in 1863, hangs on the wall.

■ **The Main Hall:** This was added on in 1867. It is the most grand room, freshly renovated in the summer of 2001, with stunning ceiling decoration, three chandeliers and Corinthian style pillars. From the gilded, ornate leaved tops of these peek out elephants. The pillars themselves look as if they are made of marble, but in fact they are made from *scaglioli,* an Italian method using a wooden frame covered in plaster and painted to look like marble. On the walls are portraits of many worthies, including Queen Victoria, plus several brass plaques listing the names of Master Cutlers, Benefactors and Founders. Around the top frieze are quotations and dates referring to the history of the Cutlers. The quote from Chaucer's Canterbury Tales is there, plus a worthy recommendation by the Victorian artist, critic and writer John Ruskin, whose art gallery collection is now housed in the nearby Millennium Galleries:

*"In cutlers' ironwork we have in Sheffield the best of its kind done by English hands - unsurpassable when the workman chooses to do all he knows by that of any living nation."*

This is the room used for the Cutlers' Feast, the gathering and banquet held in Spring each year.

Above: Stork scissors, on display at Cutlers Hall

■ **The Hughes Room:**
This pale green, panelled room is dominated by a long table lined with chairs. The largest chair is for the Master Cutler of course! The doors are from the SS Olympic.
The room is named after Herbert Hughes, a law clerk for the Company who died in 1917 and his portrait hangs there. Also in the room are several trophies, including three won in 1777, 1779 and 1781 when Sheffield had a racecourse and The Bingham Challenge Shield, given for shooting.
In one cabinet are tall silver 'whistling tankards'. These had a whistle built in, to summon more beverage when the vessel was empty. This is where the expression ' to wet your whistle' comes from.

■ **The Muniment Room:** This small room was created in 1963 from a servicing area. It displays many fascinating items, including miniature cutlery, razors, Bowie knives, old wooden handled knives found in the Thames, and the **Norfolk Knife**. This incredible piece of craftsmanship has 75 implements on it. Many of the blades are acid etched with beautifully detailed scenes including Windsor and Arundel Castles and Chatsworth House. It was made as a display piece for the Great Crystal Palace Exhibition of 1851, by Sheffield firm Joseph Rodgers and Sons Ltd, of No 6 Norfolk Street, Sheffield.
Next to this is the famous **Year Knife.** This was on display in the Millennium Galleries when they first opened, but is now displayed here. Also in this room is the original wooden staff of the Beadle (right), dating from the 19th century and topped with the emblem of the Cutlers. It was replaced in 1897 by the silver one used today, made to celebrate Queen Victoria's Diamond Jubilee. Over the door is the plaster plaque from the second (1725) Cutlers' Hall, shown on the opposite page.

Right is the oldest painting in the Cutlers' Hall, from 1638. The person who painted it had probably never seen an elephant, hence it's bizarre appearance. Below is the Master Cutler's badge of office.

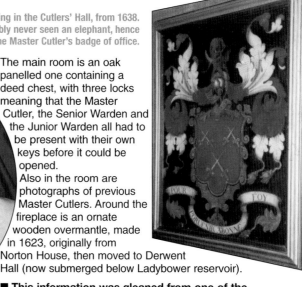

■ **The Hadfield Hall:** Named after the metallurgist Sir Robert Hadfield, who contributed much to steel making and is known as 'the father of alloy steels'. This is a large, sparsely furnished room decorated with modern murals by artist Jean Clarke, showing the history of metallurgy. There are busts of Hadfield, Sheffield poet and author John Holland and also Sheffield musician William Sterndale Bennett, who is buried in Westminster Abbey.

■ **The Master Cutler's Rooms:** The foyer is a wood panelled room, with a wood fire surround with yet another elephant's head. Two cabinets either side of the fire place contain many interesting items, including a silver Beadle's badge of authority, made in 1714, the Master Cutler's Beadle's 1896 silver mace and a model of Supertram, presented when the system was opened by Princess Anne in 1994.

The main room is an oak panelled one containing a deed chest, with three locks meaning that the Master Cutler, the Senior Warden and the Junior Warden all had to be present with their own keys before it could be opened.
Also in the room are photographs of previous Master Cutlers. Around the fireplace is an ornate wooden overmantle, made in 1623, originally from Norton House, then moved to Derwent Hall (now submerged below Ladybower reservoir).

■ **This information was gleaned from one of the tours of The Cutlers' Hall available for a small fee.**
**For enquiries ring The Cutlers' Hall on (0114) 2728456.**

## Around The Cutlers' Hall

In the picture of the Cutlers' Hall above, the **railings** which used to be around the old parish church, now the Anglican Cathedral, can be clearly seen.

### Old Public House

On the same side of Church Street as the Cutlers' Hall and just a little further towards Leopold Street, the **Stone House** pub has an old sign from 1795, when it used to be a place called White and Sons

This old post box is directly opposite the Cutler's Hall, in front of the Anglican Cathedral.

### Judge Statue

On Church Street, just along from and on the opposite side of the road from the Cutlers' Hall, is an ornate old Victorian building with an imposing statue of a judge on the outside. This was built in the late 1800's as offices for a firm of solicitors. It is called **Cairns Chambers** after Hugh McCalmont Cairns, a lawyer who was a Lord Chancellor in Prime Minister Disraeli's government. His statue stands under an elaborate canopy.

On the same building is a lovely **sundial** bearing the words 'Tempus Fugit', Latin for time flies.

# Beauchief Abbey

**In Beauchief are the ruins of a 12th century Abbey. Legend says it was founded to ease the conscience of a man involved in the martyrdom of Thomas à Becket...**

Just off Abbey Lane, between Chesterfield Road and Abbeydale Road South are the ruins of the building that gave this road its name. The abbey was founded about 1176 by a man called Robert Fitzranulph, Lord of Alfreton, Norton and Marnham. Some people said he felt implicated in the murder of Archbishop Thomas à Becket, in Canterbury Cathedral, on December 29, in the year 1170.

## The martyrdom of Thomas

The king in 1170, Henry II, was involved in an argument with his Archbishop, Becket, about the rights and privileges of the church. Henry was in Normandy and was becoming more and more exasperated with Becket, who was, he felt, insulting his authority from his seat at Canterbury Cathedral back in England. At last the king could stand it no more and tradition has it that he said to his knights,

*" ...not one of those cowards whom I feed at my table will deliver me from a priest who insults me!"*

Four knights that heard this outburst, Reginald Fitzurse, Hugh de Morville, William de Tracy and Richard Le Bret, decided to try and win favour. They left for England, burst into Canterbury Abbey as Vespers were sung and killed Thomas à Becket with sword blows.

Although Robert Fitzranulph, founder of Beauchief Abbey, was not one of the murderers, time has got him involved in some way. Perhaps he had known of the plot and did nothing to stop it. Whatever the reason, he felt guilty enough to found the abbey and become a canon. There is, however, no proof of any connection. Perhaps the fact that he founded the abbey and then became a canon himself fuelled the rumours.

*Map: Ecclesall Wood, Hutcliffe Wood, ABBEYDALE ROAD SOUTH, ABBEY LANE, Golf course, BEAUCHIEF ABBEY*

## The building of the abbey

The Abbey was dedicated to St Thomas the Martyr and the Virgin Mary. Thomas à Becket had been canonised in 1173 after miracles were said to have been associated with him.

The occupants of the abbey lived by the order of St Augustine and were known as the white canons because of their white habits.

They had come there from nearby Welbeck and were ordained priests living together in a monastic way.

The abbey was said to have covered an acre, being 180ft long. The name Beauchief means 'beautiful headland', given because of the wooded outcrop in the area and this gave the abbey its name.

The church ran east and west, with cloisters to the south, the refectory or dining room on the south of the cloisters and the chapter house to the east of the cloisters.

The chapter house had columns and vaulting and stone benches for sitting on during the meetings. Just outside, by the doorway two stone coffins were found with bones still intact. The bones were both of men. One was tall and youngish, the other short and old. They were probably abbots.

## Around the Abbey

The abbey was handed over to Henry VIII's commissioners on February 4, 1536, when the king was seizing land and property from the church during the dissolution of the monasteries. Beauchief was bought by Sir Nicholas Strelley, from Strelley in Nottinghamshire. The estate stayed in the Strelley family until 1648, then passed to the Pegge family by marriage. The abbey was already in ruins by this time, and stones were re-used to build the present chapel in 1662, using the still standing west tower.

### Beauchief Hall

This was also the time that the nearby Beauchief Hall was built, in 1671, also using stones from the old abbey. It stands about half a mile up the lane from the abbey. The most impressive features are a sweep of stone steps and stone balustrading.

The hall once belonged to De La Salle College but is now a privately owned business property.

After the Strelley family, the estate went to the Pegge family, then the Burnell family from Nottinghamshire, who were their heirs. It was supposed to be a marital home for Mr Pegge's son Gervase, but he died before the wedding and the hall was left unfurnished for 160 years.

The estate was then bought by a Mr Frank Crawshaw, who gifted it to the city in 1931. It is said that Mr Crawshaw was made an offer by an American who wished to buy the abbey and ship it to the USA, but he refused to sell.

### The abbey chapel today

Though the present small chapel was built from the old abbey in 1662, the tower dates from the 14th century. It is a third shorter than it was originally. The arched stone doorways are from other parts of the abbey. The one on the left is in the round Norman style and the one on the right is in a later, more pointed early English style. The lines of the original roof can be seen on the sides of the tower. On the walls inside the chapel are large tablets and wooden panels, or hatchments, coats of arms that were displayed at funerals

Detail of a stained glass window in the Abbey Chapel

**The Psalm board**

There is an unusual psalm board in the chapel, with a cherub on one side and a coat of arms on the back.

Also in the church are seventeenth century wooden box pews, which provided private sitting compartments for the lord of the manor, servants, farm workers etc.

A fireplace is now hidden behind plaster, but the chimney can be seen from outside.

In the large east window is an oval of painted glass, probably eighteenth century. This was unfortunately broken but was repaired by one of the past caretakers.

During excavations in the early 1920's some human remains were found under the high altar of the old abbey. They are thought to be those of it's remorseful founder, Robert Fitzranulph.

**One of the wall plaques**

A view of some of the wooden box pews

Right: Remains of a pillar from the original abbey

## A sad end for the gamekeeper

In the churchyard there is an interesting gravestone under the east window. It is for John Fox, who died April 10th, 1758, aged 37 years and of John, son of John and Hannah Fox who died on September 21st, 1781, aged 27 years. The inscription tells of his sorry end:

*A gamekeeper I was at Beauchief Hall;*
*At Dore my fatal gun caused me to fall,*
*Which made a speedy passage through my head*
*And sent me to the mansions of the dead.*

*Repent in time consider mortal man,*
*Thy race extends no farther than a span.*
*Man like the flower that in the morning sown,*
*Before the night is withered and cut down.*

A view of the abbey chapel in late winter sunshine

## The White Canons

The canons living at Beauchief Abbey were from an order known as the Premonstratensians. This order was founded by St. Norbert at Premontre, near Laon in Northern France.

This order was not well represented in England. It was founded in the twelfth century. As mentioned, the canons lived under the rules of St Augustine, intended for monks to help serve in the parish as well as singing daily offices in the abbey.

At Beauchief there were probably twelve to fifteen canons, an abbot and also lay brothers, who were not fully ordained but helped with duties. Near the abbey are the fish ponds and a monks well, which provided food and drink.

Charcoal was made from the trees in Hutcliffe Wood.

There was also a smithy for working iron.

The canons owned water mills on the River Sheaf and corn mills near Bradway and Ecclesall. It was this mill that gave the area its name - Millhouses.

The canons would have been educated men from good families, also perhaps working as teachers as well as priests. They would have employed others to work the estate mills and smithy etc.

Decoration on one of the old abbey arches

## Services at the abbey chapel

**1st, 3rd and 5th Sundays of the month:**
Evensong at 3p.m.
**2nd and 4th Sundays of the month:**
Holy Communion at 11a.m.
*The 1662 Book of Common Prayer is always used.*

**Telephone: (0114) 2745000 for further information**

## Ecclesall Woods

Near Beauchief Abbey are the lovely Ecclesall Woods. As well as being full of beauty, shelter and wildlife, woods have been a long important source of building timber, whitecoal and charcoal. Tree bark was also used in the leather tanning process. Smaller branches and twigs were used for basket making, besoms and furniture.

Woods used to be divided into smaller ones, called coppices. In a coppice wood the trees would all be cut back to ground level and the branches would then grow from the base with more vigour. In Ecclesall woods some of the internal boundaries, in the form of winding low banks, can still be seen. These would probably have had walls or hedges on them making it easier to divide up the areas.

Within the woods are many depressions in the ground that are usually on sloping ground near a stream. These could have been used to make whitecoal. This is kiln dried wood that was used as fuel in water powered lead smelting processes. There would also have been many flattened areas, now hard to spot, where charcoal stacks were made. Wood charcoal is made from charring wood at a very slow, controlled rate. Charcoal stacks were covered in earth to keep in the heat. The wood was left

**FRANCIS COLLEY & SONS,**
MARKET PLACE,
**SHEFFIELD,**
TANNERS, CURRIERS & LEATHER MERCHANTS;
MANUFACTURERS OF
CURRIED LEATHER DRIVING BELTS,
ENGINE BUTTS, STRAP BUTTS, SOLE BUTTS, HARNESS LEATHER.
Dealers in WALRUS, HIPPOPOTAMUS, and all kinds of LEATHER used in IRON, CUTLERY, SILVER and METAL MANUFACTURES.
Tannery—Meersbrook, SHEFFIELD.

**An advert for a tanning business.** Note the exotic sources of leather! The lettering on the **old tannery at Chesterfield Road,** Meersbrook, can still be seen.

to burn for 24-30 hours. The kiln needed to be watched constantly so charcoal burners lived on the site of the work, in the woods. The Charcoal was then burnt as fuel producing the intense heat necessary for forging metals.

One of these wood colliers or charcoal burners met a sad end. The grave of

*Ecclesall Woods are carpeted with bluebells in the spring*

George Yardley sits in the trees, within railings. It can be found just off Whirlowdale Road, on the Beauchief side.

The stone reads:

*"In memory of George Yardley, wood collier, he was burnt to death in his cabbin on this place, October 11th 1786 William Brooke, salesman, David Glossop, gamekeeper¹, Thomas Smith, beesome maker Sampson Brookshaw, innkeeper."*

## The Dore Stone

In the old village centre of Dore, on what remains of the village green, stands a stone. This marks the spot where, in AD 829, King Ecgbert of Wessex accepted the submission of King Eanred of Northumberland. This meant that King Ecgbert became overlord of all England.

The land at this time was divided into three counties, Wessex, Mercia and Northumberland.

The borders of Northumberland came as far as Meersbrook and passed through Dore. Over that border was known as Mercia. Dore was on the Mercia, Northumbria border. The borders were marked by rivers, the River Sheaf, the Meers Brook and the Limb Brook.

Ecgbert, whose name means 'Bright Sword' wanted to take Northumberland and marched to the border at Dore. The name Dore, in fact, comes from the Anglo Saxon word DOR, a pass or entrance into a kingdom. It was expected there would be a fight, but

Eanred gave in peacefully and Ecgbert was declared King of all the land, England.

It was probable that Eanred came peacefully to submit and join with Ecgbert, as he needed help to stand up to the invaders from across the sea, from Scandinavia and they stood a better chance united.

In The Anglo Saxon Chronicles, this event is listed:

**829** *"The eighth (King) was Ecgbryht, King of Wessex and this Ecgbryht led troops to Dore against the Northumbrians. They offered him submission and a treaty; and with that they parted."*

The memorial stone is sandstone, with a plaque of black granite in the shape of a Saxon shield. It was erected in 1968 to remember this historic event. The plaque says

*"King Ecgbert of Wessex led his army to Dore in the year AD 829 against King Eanred of Northumbria by whose submission King Ecgbert became first overlord of all England."*

The dragon represents Ecgbert's tribal emblem.

# Fulwood Old Chapel

## Near one of the Sheffield's favourite parks, at Fulwood, is an old chapel, still used for worship today...

After a walk through Whiteley Woods, stopping off for a cuppa at Forge Dam cafe, it is worth a short detour up the winding path that leads around the back of the cafe to see the pretty little chapel of the old village of Fulwood.

### Beginnings

Fulwood Old Chapel, on Whiteley Lane, was founded in 1728, and built in 1729. The man who provided for this event was called William Ronksley, who was born nearby, at Fulwood Head.

In the 17th century, the village of Fullwood was quite isolated and still separate from Sheffield.

The pretty Fulwood Old Chapel and (left) a stone plaque from the front of the building

William Ronksley was educated at Sheffield Grammar School and later worked as a schoolmaster in the village of Hathersage. He died a bachelor in 1724.

In his will he left the sum of £400 plus interest accumulated on it to erect a chapel for the village for the use of 'Protestant Dissenters". Before this chapel was built the Dissenters used the Upper Chapel on Norfolk Street in the city centre.

The first minister was called Jeremiah Gill. When Gill died in 1758, ministers from the Upper Chapel supplied Fulwood until 1798 when a new reverend took over there.

In 1808, the chapel lost money put aside for paying for minister, due to a bank failing.

There have been times when the chapel has been left unused.

The daughter of Samuel Plimsoll, the 'Sailor's Friend' is buried here according to an article in the Weekly Independent of December 5, 1908. Plimsoll and family had lived at Whiteley Wood Hall, which was nearby and worshipped at the chapel.

Next to the chapel is an old house, built in 1754, where the minister lived. The old school room, also next to the chapel. is now used as a meeting room.

It is also used by the Junior Church.

In 1934 the building was renovated, with electric lighting installed. It was reopened as a Unitarian chapel, used by independent minded religious seekers. The first Unitarian service was on Sunday May 6th, 1934.

Fulwood Old Chapel is now a Grade II listed building.

### The stocks

Outside the chapel are some old stocks, used to hold people in as punishment. These where moved to the present site when the road was widened in 1929. Part of the chapel burial ground was also taken with the road.

The recreation ground opposite used to be a quarry. The changes to make it a recreation ground were made in 1951, to commemorate the Festival of Britain.

Near the chapel used to be Fulwood Spa. The location of this is now lost, but many used to come here to take the waters.

Old stocks outside the chapel

To find out more about the chapel, contact them at:
e mail: info@fulwood-old-chapel.org.uk
web site: www.fulwood-old-chapel.org.uk

# Forge Dam

Opposite Fulwood Chapel, across the grass and down a cobbled path, lies Forge Dam. This is a favourite spot for many, and is on the route of beautiful walks. It is about 2 miles from Endcliffe Park if you come from Hunter's Bar direction. Here is found a bunting decked haven of butties, ice creams and welcome cups of tea - the Forge Dam Cafe. The cafe is on the site of an old forge, where the cafe name originates.

Forge Dam Cafe

Behind the cafe can be seen an arch that is all that remains of the old works. This point is where the entrance for the shaft of the old water wheel was. In front of the cafe, providing soothing water sounds for people sitting at the tables, is the weir, with a stepped slope. At the top right is a post for the shuttle gate. This gate can be opened up and down, hence the name, and used to regulate the amount of water in the dam, allowing it to be emptied and the level controlled.

There were around 20 mills in a 4 mile area along this stream, or small river, The Porter. Forge Dam is a 'cross valley' dam, stopping water across all of the valley. It also silts up easily.

The first known mention of this dam was in 1779, when it was owned by Thomas Boulsover.

Another dam stood just east of here but is now a filled in grassy area. The old forge operated until 1887.

Heading from the Forge Dam cafe is a lovely walk back townwards to Endcliffe Park and Hunter's Bar.

## The mill waters

A weir was built to deflect water into a reservoir or dam, via a channel called a **head race** or head **goit.** The dam was parallel to the river but at a higher level. Water was fed from the dam on to a water wheel then flowed away via a **tail goit** or tail race to join the river downstream.

Wheels where the water was falling down on to the wheel from high up were called **overshot** wheels. The one at Shepherds Wheel is an overshot example. On some the water hit the wheel mid way down and were called **breast shot** wheels and on some it was very low and went under the wheel to turn it. These were called **undershot** wheels.

## Natural beauty

The Porter Valley would once have been echoing to the sounds of industry from all the mills and forges.

Now it is a haven for walkers and wildlife. Many birds can be spotted, including jays. Wild flowers line the banks and carpet the woods with colour.

In spring there are Ramsons or Wild Garlic dotting the woods, lending a pungent aroma and the gold of Lesser Celandines mixes with white and delicate Wood Anemones.

Wild Garlic or Ramsons

Back of the cafe showing the arch where the wheel was

## Wiremill Dam

Past the playground and across the lane, the public footpath runs alongside the goit (or headrace) to another dam, Wiremill Dam, which is about a quarter of a mile further on. This was built in 1761 by Thomas Boulsover and has the longest headrace in the city. It is fed by the weir below Forge Dam through the small arch shaped culvert seen at the right hand side. There used to be two dams here, but they were opened up into one big one sometime around the 1820's. In the 1860's it was used by a firm called Ramsdens and turned into a wire mill, which is where the name today comes from. In spring, hundreds of froglets can be seen around Wiremill dam, clambering down the steps. It is also a favourite spot for fishing. You may be lucky enough to spot a heron or a kingfisher too.

The weir with steps, opposite the Forge Dam Cafe

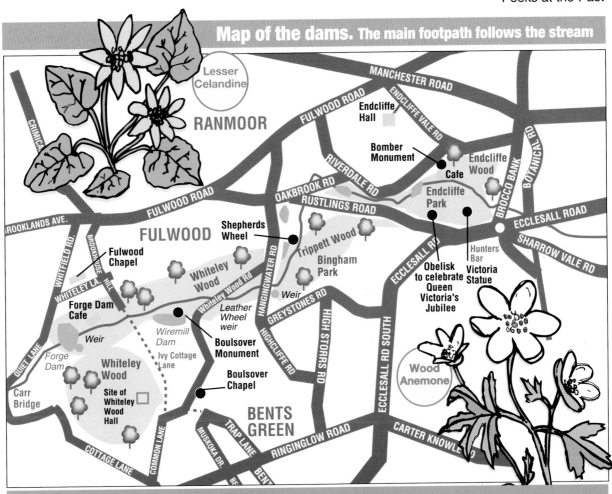

## Map of the dams. The main footpath follows the stream

## Thomas Boulsover

At the side of Wiremill dam is a stone monument with a corniced top and an arch in each of its two faces. Carved on the stone on one arch is an elephant and a shield with three pairs of crossed swords, the crest of the Cutlers' Company. This is a reminder of the importance of the site and is a memorial to Thomas Boulsover. The monument has a stone scroll which says "1705 TB 1788" and in the arch is a bronze plaque which reads

*"This memorial was erected partly of the stones from a mill built near this place by Thomas Boulsover, the inventor of Sheffield Plate. Born 1705, died 1788.*

*He carried on his industries here and resided at Whiteley Wood Hall from 1762 until his death. Erected by David Flather Master Cutler 1926-27"*

Boulsover is a man who helped shape the industrial history of Sheffield. He made a chance discovery that he could fuse silver on to copper, therefore making a cheaper product that looked like silver but was in fact just coated with it. He was working as a cutler in 1742 when he was repairing a knife handle. This had parts made of both copper and silver when he wrongly over-heated the metals and they fused together, giving him his revolutionary plate idea.

**Boulsover memorial**

Boulsover's process reigned supreme until electroplating was invented. He produced silver plated articles by rolling ingots of silver coated copper into sheets. He did not patent this discovery, however and it was soon copied.

Boulsover specialised in making small articles, such as buttons and snuff boxes. He built his rolling mill and forge on the River Porter at Whiteley Woods, at the place now called Wiremill Dam. The works buildings were below the dam, at the back of the monument.

The firm where he was working when he discovered silver plate is said to have stood near where the stage door of the Crucible Theatre is now, but some dispute this is the correct place. A monument to Boulsover can be found at this site in Tudor Square. It was made by artist Richard Perry in 1991.

Further up Whiteley Wood Road, near its junction with Trap Lane, is a Methodist Chapel built in 1789 by Boulsover's daughters, in his memory.

**Above is the chapel built by his daughters. Right: a plaque from the chapel**

## More old wheel sites

Crossing over Whiteley Wood Road as you walk on, the weir of Leather Wheel is on the right of the continuing footpath. This was a small grinding wheel, built around the 1750's. The dam pond was on the other side of the path, just a little ahead of you. The buildings were a little further along what is now the path, on a flattened landscaped area.

### Shepherd's Wheel

This is a well preserved example of a water powered grinding shop, or 'hull'. Little is known about its early days, but it could be the same wheel mentioned in a will in 1584, and referred to as the Potar Wheel (as in Porter, the river it stands on).

There are two workshops or 'hulls', both powered by one overshot wheel which is still there at the back of the buildings. It is 18ft (5.5m) in diameter and six feet (2m) wide. The spokes

Old mill stones re-used as steps at Shepherd's Wheel

hub and rims are made of cast iron. As the wheel turned it also turned a large gear wheel inside the building, which then in turn moved a large wooden drum, so moving leather belts which then turned the grind-stones. At least 18 grindstones could be operated off this one wheel, mainly to sharpen knives. The grinder sat astride a wooden 'horsing' over the grindstone. The stones only lasted up to eight weeks and then were replaced, with the old ones being sold off to workers who used smaller stones. Later the lands, and so the wheel, came into the estates of the Duke of Norfolk.

The first mention of a wheel here is in 1566, in the will of a man called Roger Barnsley.

The name Shepherd's wheel is from one of the tenants, Edward Shepherd, who operated it in the second half of the 18th century. He employed ten grinders. The grinding wheel itself was used up until as late as the 1930's, when demonstrations were given at Bank Holidays. By the 1940's it was in a bad way and was almost demolished, though luckily it was repaired instead. Now it is owned by the council and open to the public most weekends in summer.

There are other wheel sites along this valley including Ibbotson Wheel, whose dam is now a water fowl home. A book telling of these water powered industries, edited by David Crossley, and called Water Power on the Sheffield Rivers (isbn 0 950660124) is a very informative guide. Friends of the Porter Valley also organise guided walks on the history and wildlife of the area.

The wheel at the back of Shepherd's Wheel

Looking inside Shepherd's Wheel at the conditions the grinders worked in is a harsh reminder that even though it is a scenic place now, the grinders would have been hard at work, with little time to enjoy the view. They would be inside the dusty workshops risking terrible diseases like Grinder's Asthma. This was caused by inhalation of stone and metal dust. In the 1830's a grinder's life expectancy could be as little as 30 or so. Also everpresent was the danger of the grinding wheel cracking and causing injury or death as the pieces shot out. Eyes also suffered, with all the dust and steel particles. Sadly many of the grinders were resigned to dying young and it seems from this extract from The Life of Ebenezer Elliott (written by John Watkins, his son in Law), that they felt that this was the only way there would always be enough work...

"The mills on the stream and the weirs belonging to them made a succession of beautiful landscapes. We looked in at one of those mills and saw an old man of thirty, a grinder. He said they seldom reached forty... yet if they prolonged their lives, there would not be enough work for them all and they preferred to die of the disease rather than of starvation."

A poem by Ebenezer Ellott (The Corn Law Rhymer):

### THE GRINDER

There draws the grinder his laborious breath;
There, coughing, at his deadly trade he bends.
Born to die young, he fears not man nor death;
Scorning the future, what he earns he spends.
Debauch and riot are his bosom friends....
Bid science on his cheek prolong the bloom,
He will not live! He seems in haste to gain
the undisturbed asylum of the tomb,
And, old at two-and-thirty, meets his doom!"

### Friends of The Porter Valley

This group was formed in 1994 to "preserve and enhance the natural and historical characteristics of the Porter Valley". They carry out occasional conservation work and liaison with the council over plans, improvements etc. Contact secretary Flora Owen on (0114) 230 1345 for details or look up their website: **www.portervalley.fsnet.co.uk**

**Right: Walking alongside the dam at Shepherd's Wheel on one of the guided talks and walks by The Friends of The Porter Valley**

## More of interest in Endcliffe Park

Memorial to the crashed bomber

### Site of a crashed bomber

Beyond the stepping stones, across the River Porter and near the park cafe is a monument to the 10 man crew of a Flying Fortress bomber, the Mi Amigo. This had been damaged in Germany in 1944, during the Second World War and was returning home to base when it crashed here on February 22nd. All the men died in the crash. They had made great efforts to avoid the nearby houses.

A wreath is laid here every year.

This stone, near the park cafe and toilets, tells of the giving of this recreation ground to commemorate Queen Victoria's jubilee

ENDCLIFFE PARK LODGE

This building was erected sometime between 1894 and 1897. It became a lodge and refreshment room in 1933. Since 1999 it has been the Ranger cabin for the Western Area Ranger Team.

## Old Monuments in the Park

### The Jubilee Monument

This stone needle,10 metres or so high, was erected to commemorate Queen Victoria's jubilee in 1887. It originally stood in Town Hall Square.

When it was moved here to the park in 1905 it was replaced with a statue of Queen Victoria (see below).

It originally had four cast iron gas lamps at the corners and was designed by architects Flockton and Gibbs.

The monument when it stood in Town Hall Square

### Statue of Queen Victoria

This statue was the one that replaced the Jubilee Memorial at Town Hall Square. It too was later moved to Endcliffe Park, in 1930 and now stands near the Hunter's Bar entrance and the lodge. It was made by artist Alfred Turner in 1905 and shows Queen Victoria, crowned and holding an orb and sceptre. The stone pedestal bears a statue of a man with a hammer (Labour) and a woman and two children (maternity).

An inscription on the statue says "Erected by citizens of Sheffield in memory of a great queen."

The statues of Maternity and Labour

The Queen Victoria statue

# Bradfield & the flood

**Around midnight on March 11, 1864, a dam at Dale Dike reservoir burst, sending millions of gallons of water crashing down the Loxley Valley, taking more than 200 lives with it.**

A flood level marker

SHEFFIELD FLOOD 11·3·1864

Sheffield in 1864 was a dirty, ugly place, with a population of around 185,000. Disease and ill health were rife, and memories of the cholera epidemic of thirty years before were still raw. Shortage of water was one of the problems and a grand new scheme was underway to build reservoirs and provide fresh water for all. These would also give more power to the growing number of mills. Dale Dike reservoir was part of this plan.

## The building of the dam

It was an enormous undertaking. Building at Dale Dike began on January 1, 1859. A trench 60ft deep and a sloping embankment of stone and earth almost 100ft high in the centre was built, stretching for a quarter of a mile across the valley.

To help control water volume, twin 18inch wide pipes were passed through the embankment at a depth of 9ft, with valves on them to release pressure. The reservoir was designed to hold 700 million gallons of water, which put a force of 3 million tons on the embankment.

## A small crack

March 1864 had been very wet, meaning the River Don was already high. Out on the moors beyond Bradfield, the newly finished Dale Dike reservoir was also full to the brim.

At 5.30 in the morning of March 11, workmen noticed a crack in the newly built dam The crack was 12 feet from the top of the embankment, and about 50 yards long, and wide enough to stick a pocket knife in. A little later it was wide enough to take two adult fingers. Rain lashed down and a gale was blowing as the workers decided to send a young lad to fetch the supervisor, John Gunson, from his home, the resident engineer's house next to the Water Board offices at Division Street, Sheffield, eight miles away.

Some villagers at nearby Dam Flask village had heard rumours of a crack and headed for higher ground, with belongings and livestock. Gunson was very concerned when he finally reached the dam after a hurried ride. He decided to let out some water through the pipes by lifting the sluice gates...but it was too late.

## The dam bursts

At 11.35pm, water began foaming over the embankment and the men ran for their lives. The sound was said to be like a thousand steam engines letting off steam at once as the water crashed through the man made barrier towards those helpless in its path.

At Low Bradfield, Joseph Dawson and his family had a narrow escape. Joseph saw the water rising about his house and ran to the bedrooms. There was no way out, except through the window. Quick thinking and a ladder placed from the window to a high bank at the side of the house enabled them to scramble to safety. Other people escaped drowning by smashing holes through their bedroom ceilings and climbing on to the roof.

The people with forethought to leave Dam Flask village had been wise. Buildings there were washed away in an instant. Inns and cottages were smashed by thick mud and boulders as the water thundered over them. Mills were swept to oblivion, along with the workers on night shifts. Massive machines were smashed like toys. Fires from forges were extinguished along with lives. At Malin Bridge, 94 or so of the villagers were killed.

By 12.30 am the flood waters had reached Hillsborough Bridge. A gruesome flotsam of debris and the bodies of humans and animals was deposited here as the land flattened out a little. At Owlerton a lake formed, also full of the bodies of people and cattle.

### The dreadful toll of the flood

| | |
|---|---|
| 73 men | A total of 240 dead |
| 57 women | £500,000 worth of property lost |
| 67 boys | |
| 43 girls | |

## On towards Sheffield

Leaving a path of death and destruction behind it in the Loxley Valley, the water, still around 15ft high, crashed into the Don Valley, towards Sheffield.

At the Ball Street Bridge, debris jammed and eventually broke the bridge, releasing the pent up water into Kelham Island. Chimneys fell and furnaces steamed out in the roar.

At the south end of Kelham Island were some cottages. Here lived John Eaton and his family. As the water rushed towards them, John tried to save his pig, but was swept away and drowned. His wife tried to save him, but she was drowned too.

In the workhouse, a four storey converted cotton mill on Kelham Street, there were no casualties as everyone was moved to the top floor. Later the building was used to shelter the homeless and store bodies to be identified.

Not realising the extent of the tragedy up river, 200 or so people stood watching as debris washed under Lady's Bridge. The bridge was bashed and shaken, but survived unbroken.

At last the torrent was slowed. The swollen River Don had spread wreckage and bodies through Rotherham, Mexbrough and towards Doncaster, 27 miles from the reservoir.

The scene at Lady's Bridge

## News of the tragedy spreads

The next day the scale of the tragedy was clear and people were in total shock. The presses at the Sheffield Telegraph had run all night to bring the facts and stories of what had happened. Hundreds were dead and police began moving bodies. The mayor, Thomas Jessop, ordered the soldiers stationed at Hillsborough Barracks to be on guard to prevent looting.

People further afield heard of the flood and over the next short period over 150,000 visitors came to see it for themselves.

Photographers and artists had a field day, capturing the twisted stones and mill wheels, uprooted trees and scenes of sadness. The flood was probably the first major catastrophe to be captured in photographs. Disaster tourism is unfortunately nothing new. Postcards were produced as mementos and people posed by the wreckage for posterity.

The dispute over who was to blame and the problem of insurance claims went on for months. Sadly life was only valued in terms of earning power. A piano was valued more than a child who was too young to work.

## Flood reminders

Today the terrible height of the flood levels are hard to imagine. Some buildings bear plaques that mark the water level. These take the form of mill wheels and bear the date of the tragedy, They can be seen on the Old Blue Ball public house, the Hillsborough Barracks supermarket entrance and other places.

A plaque, erected in 1991 by Bradfield Historical Society stands next to a footpath near Dale Dike. Conifers hide the site of the old embankment, but small stones bearing the letters CLOB can be spotted. This stands for 'Centre Line of Old Bank".

## Literary tale of the flood

Victorian novelist Charles Reade has characters caught up in the flood in his story Put Yourself in His Place, and weaves in many of the things that really happened. He changed some names, with Sheffield becoming Hillsborough. Malin Bridge became Poma Bridge, Owlerton became Allerton and the Dam he called Ousley. Dam Flask kept its own name. He doesn't do the area at the time any favours however!:

"Hillsborough, though built on one of the loveliest sites in England, is perhaps the most hideous in creation.

All ups and downs and back slums. ...But worst of all the city is pockmarked with public-houses and bristles with high round chimneys....More than one crystal stream runs sparkling down the valleys and enters the town; but they soon get defiled and creep through it heavy charged with dyes, clogged with putridity and bubbling with poisonous gases, till at last they turn to mere ink, stink and malaria and people the churchyards as they crawl."

IN MEMORY OF THOSE WHO LOST THEIR LIVES OWING TO THE BREACHING OF DALE DYKE RESERVOIR ON MARCH 11TH 1864. ERECTED BY: BRADFIELD HISTORICAL SOCIETY FROM PUBLIC DONATIONS.

He describes the beginning of the flood thus:

"the rent in the top of the embankment spread - deepened- yawned terrifically- and the pent up lake plunged through and sweeping away at once the centre of the embankment, rushed, roaring and hissing, down the valley, an avalanche of water, whirling great trees up by the roots and sweeping huge rocks away and driving them, like corks, for miles."

**These illustrations below and left were drawn especially for the Sheffield newspaper by their 'special artist'.**

# Hillsborough Barracks

This imposing building, with its castellated walls stands in the heart of busy Hillsborough on Langsett Road, with trams gliding past its historic walls. Built in 1850, it was known as the New Barracks, as it replaced an older building also on Langsett Road, but further towards the town centre.

Where it stands was once a more countrified spot, as described in Pawson and Brailsford's 1862 guide to Sheffield, stating that these barracks, "amongst the finest in the kingdom", stood quite in the outskirts of the town, on a salubrious spot and commanding magnificent views of the surrounding scenery."

The Barracks had its own chapel, and headstones from this can be seen now the yard has been opened up for the shopping developments, and they have been repositioned on the wall. One soldier was at Waterloo. Another was hit by a train at the end of the inclined tunnel on the Midland Line. His stone has a rather gruesome epitaph to indicate this.

The Barracks spent part of its life as Burdall's, as a sign on the wall testifies, but now contains shops and a supermarket.

On the wall near the supermarket entrance, above the rows of trolleys, is a marker for the level the Sheffield Flood waters reached.

The Barracks today.

INFANTRY SOLDIERS QUARTERS

Above is the old Burdall's sign painted on a wall. Below are some of the gravestones for soldiers, to be seen at the side of the chapel (right).

SACRED to the Memory of GEORGE RAYNOR, late of the 1st or Kings Dragoon Guards, who departed this Life on the 3rd Day of June 1834, aged 54 Years. He served in the above Corps 31 Years, 20 of which as a Non-commissioned Officer, and highly distinguished Himself in the ever memorable Battle of WATERLOO. This St...

THIS STONE IS ERECTED IN MEMORY OF JOHN KIDD, WHO LOST HIS LIFE AT THE END OF THE INCLINED TUNNEL ON THE MIDLAND LINE AT SHEFFIELD, DECEMBER 8th 1846, AGED 29 YEARS. Here lieth the body of John Kidd, In eternal realms his soul is hid; A railway engine did him kill, And crushed his poor head so ill.

SACRED To the Memory of CAPTN GILL late of the 24th Regt of Foot, Barrack Master of Shef'd who departed this Life the 7th of April 1850, aged 54 Years.

## Bradfield Church

The picturesque church of St Nicholas stands in a commanding position on the hills of High Bradfield. It is the last resting place of many victims of the Sheffield Flood.

The area is full of history. By the end of the 11th century the Normans were living in the area. It was probably they who built the motte (mound of earth) and bailey (a wooden palisade usually with a tower), still visible as a large mound and now called Bailey Hill. It stands to the north-west of the church.

The original stone church is thought to have been built around 1109 by the Lovetot family. They were Lords of the Manor of Hallamshire. This would have been a very simple building. Surviving parts of the Norman church include two round pillars in the north arcade.

Later, in the 1480's, the church was rebuilt, the new structure being much bigger than before. The church was restored in 1870 by a Reverend Gatty.

During the Reformation and the Civil War, much of the finery, such as glass and statues, were removed. Later it was altered again. Much of the present wooden furniture was added in the 19th century.

The saxon cross in the north aisle, opposite the main door, was found buried in a field at Low Bradfield in 1870. It is thought to date from the 9th century.

There are also some lovely roof bosses, including John the Baptist's head on a plate and a fine 'Green Man.' He is the second boss in from the front door. The church also has some fine stained glass, including one window containing salvaged fragments of original 15th century Medieval glass from the church.

The oak lectern is in the shape of an eagle.

Carved in New York by an American firm, it won a prize at an exhibition in Philadelphia in 1876 before it was purchased by a Canadian with some Bradfield connections.

**The old cross**

**Green man boss**

**A music festival is held here every June. The church has a fine choral tradition and has choral services each Sunday (10.30am) and evensong (6.30pm) for details ring Reverend Canon Trevor Page: (0114) 285 1225**

**The watch house**

A slate plaque in the south aisle commemorates the Sheffield Flood:

To remember the breach of the Dale Dyke embankment on 11 March 1864 when at least 240 people died. Let not a flood overwhelm me or the depths swallow me up.

The plain Norman font is thought to have been made and donated by the Cistercian monks of Roche Abbey in the 12th century.

The watch house by the main gates was built to look out for grave robbers in search of fresh corpses to steal and sell for medical research.

Towards the top left of the graveyard, looking from the back of the church, is a grave for the Trickett family, who lost their lives in the Sheffield Flood. The stone reads: James Trickett, aged 39, Elizabeth Trickett, aged 36, their daughter Jemima, aged 12, their son James, aged 10 and son George, aged 6. "who perished in the great flood at Malin bridge."

"Whoe'er may be blamed for the recent distress, Our duty to God it makes none the less. Whatever be the fault this is most true, The flood is a warning to me and to you."

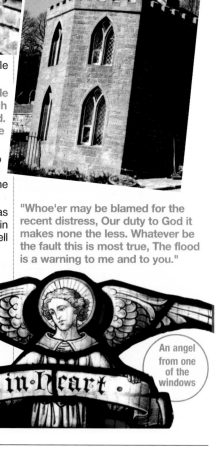

**An angel from one of the windows**

# Edward Carpenter

PHOTO: STAR ARCHIVES

*An eccentric academic once wandered Millthorpe and Bradway, raising eyebrows with his bare feet and sandals, bohemian lifestyle and aesthetic ideas...*

Many of this man's ideas were ahead of his time, including supporting the rights of women to independence and having a child without being tied to a man. He was also a poet and a mystic.

**"I heard the world-old cry of the down-trodden and outcast: I saw them advancing always to victory..."**

**After Long Ages, Toward's Democracy.**

### The Early Years

Edward Carpenter was born in Brighton on August 29, 1844 at 25 Brunswick Square. At 10 he went to Brighton College, later returning home where he lived with parents and sisters. Even in early years he was sad at the lack of life women had, saying his sisters "had absolutely nothing to do except dabble in paints and music and wander aimlessly from room to room to see if anything was going on."

After Brighton College, Edward went to Trinity Hall, Cambridge, winning a prize in 1866 for an essay on modern civilisation. This essay showed his interest in Utopian ideas, harmony and the plight of class struggle. He dreamed of education being provided for all classes of people. In May 1869 he became a deacon at the college, and expanded his love of music and writing, producing various books. His love of poetry led him to discover the work of American poet Walt Whitman.

By 1871, Carpenter felt that academic life was full of hypocrites and wanted to leave. He resigned from his curate's life and dedicated himself to poetry, with Socialist themes.

He decided he had the need to write and commit more time to the open air and manual work, to achieve the 'simplification of life'. He wanted to help educate manual workers and wrote to Walt Whitman telling him of his ideals. He began lecturing for the workers in the autumn of 1873. He taught Astronomy in Leeds, Halifax and Skipton, having a break back to Brighton in 1876 before more lectures in Nottingham and Barnsley.

In April 1877 he went to New Jersey to meet Walt Whitman and was inspired by their similar dreams of education. peace and good living standards and jobs for all. Whitman and Carpenter were both also fascinated by 'the manly love of comrades'.

Carpenter later moved to Sheffield, where he said he felt at ease with the unpretentious people. He lived at the top of Glossop Road, in rooms that he describes in his autobiography *My Days and Dreams* as "my lodging place where people were most doleful".

**"Rough in the extreme, twenty or thirty years behind other towns and very uneducated, there was yet a heartiness about them, not without shrewdness, which attracted me."**

**My Days and Dreams - talking about Sheffield people**

He was still lecturing in Sheffield, Chesterfield and York and decided to move to Chesterfield. His relationship with a friend from Cambridge, George Oates, had flowered into intimacy by this time. Carpenter had already spoken of his ideal *"my ideal love is a powerful, strongly built man, of my own age or younger, preferably of the working class."*

*"The woman soul within a man's form dwelling, (was Adam perchance like this, ere Eve from his side was drawn?)...Strange twice-born, having entrance to both worlds- Loved, loved by either sex and free of all their lore!."*

**Child of Uranus, Toward's Democracy, part IV**

### The Sheffield Socialists

Perhaps it was because Carpenter lived in South Yorkshire and Derbyshire, with more radical, working traditions than his birthplace, that he managed to sustain his beliefs and politics more than he would have in London and Cambridge. Forming a Socialist group in Sheffield merely strengthened the interest there already. There were meetings, excursions, public speaking and a favourite haunt of the Socialists was the Wentworth Cafe, which used to be on Holly Street.

Open air meetings began in 1886, at the corner of Surrey Street and Fargate, sometimes to hundreds of people.

*"Yet the smoke still lay over Sheffield. Sullenly it crawled and spread; Round the bases of the tall chimneys, over the roofs of the houses, in waves - and the city was like a city of chimneys and spires rising out of a troubled sea."* Sheffield, from Toward's Democracy. part IV.

No. 12. **England Arise!**

Four-Part Song (S.A.T.B.)                    Words and Music by E. CARPENTER.

*f* Eng - land a - rise! the long long night is o - ver, Faint in the east be -

COVER AND PAGE FROM CARPENTER'S CHANTS OF LABOUR SONG BOOK

In 1887, the Socialist group found a place to have as a meeting centre, at Scotland Street. It had been an old debtor's jail and was called the Commonwealth Cafe.

Carpenter lived in an attic at the top of the building for a year or so, above much of the city noise:

*"In the early morning at 5am there was the strident sound of the hummers and the clattering of innumerable clogs of men and girls going to their work and on till late at night there were drunken cries and shouting. Far around stretched nothing but factory chimneys and foul courts inhabited by the wretched workers."*

He spent his spare time there playing his harmonium and compiling *Chants of labour- A Song Book of the People.*

Many meetings with the unemployed were held at the cafe, which held 150 and was often overflowing. One open air demonstration at West Bar overflowed into Paradise Square.

## The communes

In 1879 one of Carpenter's students, a scythemaker called Albert Fearnehough, invited him to visit his cottage and farm at Bradway, on land owned by a man with Socialist beliefs, called Charles Fox. Albert lived there with his wife and two children. Carpenter loved it all and moved in there. He wanted to achieve his aims of 'the simplification of life.'

In 1880, Carpenter's mother died, and his father soon after in 1882, leaving some inheritance, which Carpenter used to buy a smallholding at Millthorpe, near Holmesfield. He built a house on 7 acres of land. The Fearnehough's came too, to help share the housekeeping and gardening. The nearest railway station was four miles away and visitors and admirers had to walk to the cottage. Here they became market gardeners, taking produce for sale in Sheffield and Chesterfield on a cart.

At one end of his cottage, Carpenter had a small workshop, where he made sandals for himself and his friends. He wore sandals all the time, (probably inspired by his visits abroad), and this added to his eccentric reputation, as well as his wide brimmed felt hats, loose shirts, knicker bocker type tweed suits and long stockings.

Carpenter built a little summer house by the brook in his gardens, where he did much of his writing. He used the nearby barn to put on plays, including St George and the Dragon in 1913. He also led whit sings at the local cricket club field.

The Fearnehough's left in 1893, but others took their place. One of Carpenter's closest friends was George Hukin, a razor grinder from Bath Street. He and his wife Fannie later moved to a cottage near Holmesfield to join Carpenter. Another was George Adams, an insurance collector who left his job to join the socialist community, taking up painting and sandal making.

Later Carpenter shared his home with a younger man called George Merrill. He had met Merrill in 1891, in a railway carriage from Sheffield to Totley. Merrill was from a hard background, with an unemployed father with a drink problem.

## Carpenter's 'local'

George had various jobs to make ends meet and was living at 75 Edward St in Sheffield. He moved in with Carpenter and they were very happy together. Carpenter said George made housework "an artistic pleasure". Many of the locals were dubious of the relationship. Homosexuality was still illegal then, and the Oscar Wilde trial of 1895 was in flow.

It was a testimony to Carpenter's personality and likeability that any scandal was minimal, though there were letters of protest to the Sheffield Telegraph in 1908, from an Irishman called O'Brien.

Edward and George left Millthorpe in 1922, to live in Guildford. Six years later George died, leaving a heartbroken Edward alone. Edward himself died in Guildford in 1929.

## Literary success

The influence of Carpenter's writings on Socialism, idealism and sexuality were at a height just before the First World War. His books were translated into many languages including French, Dutch, Italian, Russian, Norwegian, Spanish and Japanese. His work was also well known in Germany,

Many literary figures visited the community at Millthorpe, including W.B Yeats, E.M. Forster, Bernard Shaw and H.G. Wells. Captain Oates, later of the famous ill fated Scott expedition, also visited.

E.M. Forster is said to have written his novel Maurice after being inspired by a visit there in 1913 and the way that Carpenter and his friends expressed their homosexual feelings. Forster said of Carpenter, "He wasn't happy in the class in which he was born. He didn't revolt from a sense of duty, or to make a splash, but because he wanted to." Forster and Carpenter also shared a fascination with India. Carpenter had visited there in 1890, meditating with the religious teachers, which was adventurous travelling for the era.

Nowadays his works are not widely known, but well worth reading to rediscover the essays and poems. This man, with ideas and a lifestyle that defied the conventions of the time he was born into, had an effect on many famous names of the literary and political world and his influence should not be forgotten.

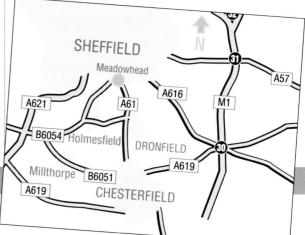

### The Royal Oak

This quaint establishment is over 300 years old and used to be a an old mill.

It was enlarged and turned into a public house in 1840. Edward Carpenter was a frequent visitor and used to play the piano in the front room there.

The Royal Oak: 2890870

### Carpenter House

The old house at Millthorpe that Edward Carpenter used to live in can be found just up the road from the Royal Oak, on Cordwell Lane.

It is now Carpenter House Bed and Breakfast accommodation.

# Around Tudor Square

This oasis of culture, set for redevelopment in the near future, contains four theatres. The most striking and historic is The Lyceum, with its cream and white facade...

On the corner of what was once Tudor Street and Arundel Street, where the lovely old Lyceum Theatre now stands, there was first the City Theatre.

## The show begins

Where the Lyceum stands was originally the site of a circus, a flimsy wooden structure let to a man called Dan Leno, which was called Leno's Varieties. Later a showman called Alexander Stacey took it over, in 1890 and it became known as Stacey's Circus. Mr Stacey, however, became more interested in the dramatic arts than circus and changed the emphasis on the entertainments, calling it Stacey's Theatre. He put on plays, which were performed there until a disaster in 1893. A show called On the Frontier had a real fire in the performance, which went a little too well and burnt down the place. Stacey then built the aformentioned City Theatre, but by 1896 he decided to sell it as it did not do as well as he had hoped.

It was bought by a syndicate, who changed the name to The Lyceum. It re-opened in January 1897 with its new name, but it was only a short season, until Easter, before it was closed for rebuilding and improvements. It was opened again, newly resplendent, in October of the same year.

The theatre designer W.G.R Sprague was employed to apply his talents. The managing director, Mr John Hart, was determined to put on more up market productions than the music halls which filled the city's other theatres.

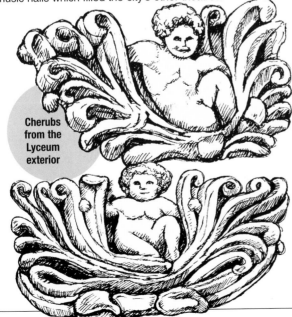

Cherubs from the Lyceum exterior

Also in October, the great Victorian actor Sir Henry Irving came to the Lyceum, with actress Ellen Terry and the rest of his company. They performed The Merchant of Venice. He became a regular visitor. He even began his farewell tour here, in 1905. He gave a farewell speech from the stage, thanking the people of Sheffield for their "sweet acts and most gracious courtesies." Less than a week later, he died.

Across from the Lyceum had stood the Theatre Royal, which burned down in 1935. The Lyceum had almost suffered the same fate in 1899. On November 6th, a fire was discovered on the stage. The fire began to spread and many came to watch. Thousands of pounds worth of damage was caused.

The Lyceum escaped damage in the war however. During the First World War, in May 1916, it had been transformed into a cinema to show a propaganda film called 'Be Prepared". During the Second World War, plays and performances carried on through the trouble and destruction.

The Lyceum Theatre, neglected in the 1970's

## Peeks at the Past

As well as plays, the Lyceum became much loved for its pantomimes. This really began when the Theatre Royal, where the pantomimes were usually held, burned down. Famous names guesting in these happy and colourful shows included Roy Hudd, Harry Secombe, Ronnie Hilton, Nat Jackley and Morecambe and Wise. Many a child was wowed by the picture book golden frame of the beautifully ornate proscenium arch, or amazed at the steep drop from the balcony.

By the fifties and sixties, with television and such vying for attention, the Lyceum dropped in popularity. The managing director, John Beamont, tried to keep it afloat by letting smaller theatre groups hire it and even putting bingo on the stage. The programmes at the time had an inscription which said

## "A city without a theatre is like a lamp without a light"

in an attempt to remind people of how vital a theatre is to the community and cultural health of a city.

The Lyceum was threatened with demolition to make way for a new theatre, but the new theatre, The Crucible, was built nearby whilst the Lyceum was still fighting on.

By March 1971 the Crucible was the place where the audience headed, The Lyceum was neglected and still in danger of being demolished to develop the land it stood on. The last pantomime had finished but a campaign to save the theatre began. Thousands signed petitions to save it, and in 1970 the actor and comedian Jimmy Jewel joined the fight, but his ideas of using it as a conference centre and doing more pantomimes with him in were a non starter.

In 1972 an announcement that the theatre would finally close and be demolished made the Hallamshire Historic Buildings group quicken their involvement for the building's preservation. They wrote to the Department of the Environment who made the Lyceum a listed building, halting its demolition. Campaigners banded together to form the Lyceum Theatre Trust and tried to raise funds for the crumbling building.

In 1977 the Lyceum was taken over by nightclub owners and turned into a venue for rock concerts, opening in 1981 after some renovation work. They stayed until January 1982, and by the middle of July the theatre had new owners promising more concerts but with the chance of opera and ballet too.

Local Band Cabaret Voltaire opened the new regime in August, with Joe Cocker the month after. But high costs and rates put an end to this idea and the theatre was closed by Christmas. January 1985 saw new plans to turn the Lyceum into a disco, restaurant and dance studio called The Academy. But licensing problems and opposition from other nightclubs put an end to this idea too.

Then the final stage of the theatre's struggle began. Chairman of South Yorkshire Opera David Heugh and their producer Norman White used their homes to raise money and buy the Lyceum for £101,000, to become a base for their opera company. They had lots of vision and enthusiasm. The Crucible and Lyceum Trusts were merged, new momentum was gained and in January 1989, the announcement was made that the Lyceum was to begin redevelopment in March. In December a £4 million grant was given from the European Regional Development Fund which boosted the project greatly. The Lyceum reopened in December 1990.

Now this rescued theatre is a jewel in the crown of the town centre, surrounded by three other theatres, the Crucible, Crucible Studio and the Library Theatre, in Tudor Square. New plans are afoot for this area, which include the library, to make this an even more special focus of culture in the city.

The lights shine on the Lyceum's cream and white edifice as audiences enter the doors full of anticipation, to watch drama, dance, music and more and be surrounded by the magical interior of this lovely architectural gem, carrying on the years of applause as the curtain rises once more.

A statue from the side of the stage

The theatre entrance canopy

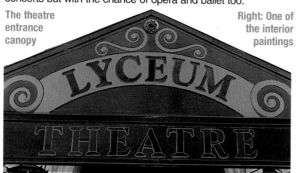

Right: One of the interior paintings

## The other theatres

As mentioned there are three other theatres in Tudor Square, The Crucible, The Crucible Studio and the Library Theatre.

### THE CRUCIBLE

This was built in 1971, appropriately named after the containers used to make steel, using the crucible method by Benjamin Huntsman.

It is famous for its 'thrust' type stage, which means three sides of the stage are open to the audience. As well as attracting many famous names its name is forever linked with Snooker.

To the right of the glass door is a plaque explaining how, in the Adelphi Hotel which stood on the site earlier, Sheffield United and Wednesday football clubs and Yorkshire County Cricket club were founded .

### THE LIBRARY THEATRE

This 262 seater theatre (shown right) is part of the library building. It is a popular venue for many theatre groups.

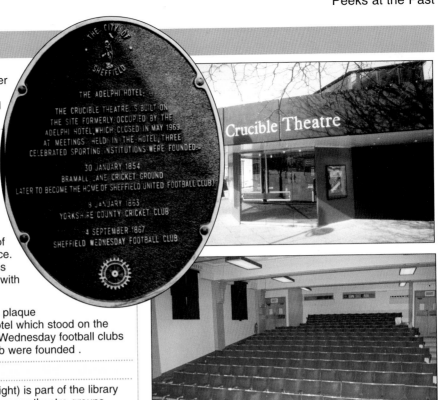

## The Library

On Surrey Street, in the nineteenth century was a building known as The Mechanics' Hall, built jointly by The Mechanics' Institute and a group known as The Lyceum Club, and used as a social institution. The Mechanics' Institute had many Sheffield worthies as members. President and Vice President were the Poets James Montgomery and Ebenezer Elliot.

There were two rooms on the ground floor of the building. Here was a library, which later became open to the public as the free Library. This opened in February 1856 as a reference library and as a lending library in June 1856.

In the 20's many libraries in the city were revamped. The free library was closed for a face lift and improvements and re-opened in June 1922.

Soon, however, it was decided a bigger grander library was needed and work began on a new building.

During the digging for the building of the new library, on December 2 1930, it was reported in the newspapers that bones of a child aged around 6 had been found. Rumours (unproven) circulated that it was the skeleton of a child that had been experimented on at a medical school which once stood on the site. Animal bones were also found.

A well, 24 feet deep, was also discovered on the site. (Telegraph and Star September 27, 1930) which had a cover of four oak beams and a stone slab.

By 1931 the foundation stone for the Art Gallery and library we know today was laid. By 1932 the first part was complete and books were being moved in. The fully completed building was opened by the then Duchess of York on July 5, 1934. The Duke was supposed to be there too but he was ill.

### The Knowledge Sculpture

In the official programme for the opening ceremony, an explanation of the sculpture which sits high on the wall of the library (shown below) was given.

It shows Knowledge being given a choice between good (an Egyptian Ankh or cross of life, symbolising this) held in one hand and evil (shown as an asp) held in the other. He is seated on the world, beneath which flow the waters under the earth.

Spirit messengers bring torches of light or inspiration.

Above is the Cosmos, shown by seven arches and stars. The tree of knowledge is symbolised by 12 fruits and leaves.

## Leader House

Thomas Leader, a silversmith, came to Sheffield around 1760. He founded a firm with Henry Tudor, which specialised in silver plate. In 1777 he leased this old house opposite the front of the library from the Duke of Norfolk. Leader's son Daniel also lived there and then, later, his grandson Robert.

In 1817 the house was sold on and eventually came to be bought by Sheffield Corporation in 1938. It was almost demolished in the 1970's to make way for the 'wedding cake' register office, but saved with help from the Hallamshire Historic Buildings Group.

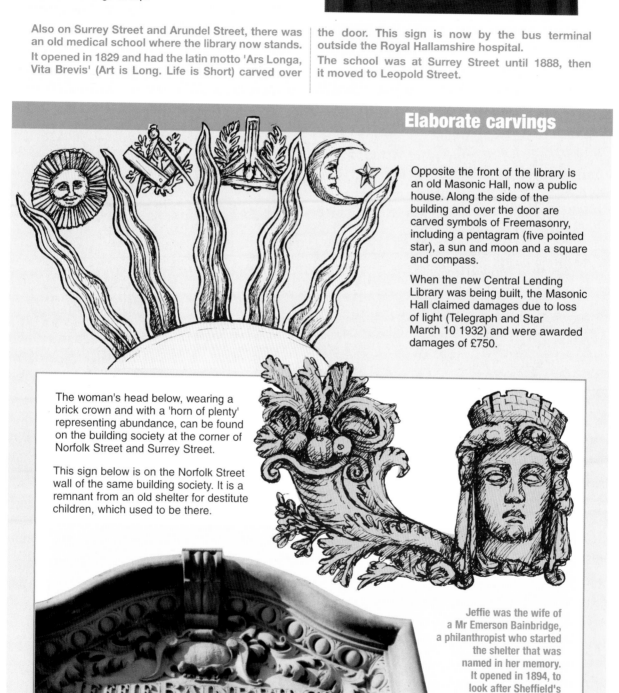

Also on Surrey Street and Arundel Street, there was an old medical school where the library now stands. It opened in 1829 and had the latin motto 'Ars Longa, Vita Brevis' (Art is Long. Life is Short) carved over the door. This sign is now by the bus terminal outside the Royal Hallamshire hospital.
The school was at Surrey Street until 1888, then it moved to Leopold Street.

## Elaborate carvings

Opposite the front of the library is an old Masonic Hall, now a public house. Along the side of the building and over the door are carved symbols of Freemasonry, including a pentagram (five pointed star), a sun and moon and a square and compass.

When the new Central Lending Library was being built, the Masonic Hall claimed damages due to loss of light (Telegraph and Star March 10 1932) and were awarded damages of £750.

The woman's head below, wearing a brick crown and with a 'horn of plenty' representing abundance, can be found on the building society at the corner of Norfolk Street and Surrey Street.

This sign below is on the Norfolk Street wall of the same building society. It is a remnant from an old shelter for destitute children, which used to be there.

Jeffie was the wife of a Mr Emerson Bainbridge, a philanthropist who started the shelter that was named in her memory. It opened in 1894, to look after Sheffield's disadvantaged children.

# Old advertisements from Norfolk Street and a grand old bank

SHEFFIELD AND SOUTH YORKSHIRE
## Permanent Building Society.

Established January 1st, 1849, and incorporated in 1875 under "The Building Societies Act, 1874."

Offices—10, NORFOLK-ST., SHEFFIELD.

ANNUAL INCOME EXCEEDS £150,000.

PRESENT BORROWING POWERS, authorised by Act of Parliament, £200,000.
On 31st Dec., 1878, the following were the balances in the Society's books:—

Due to Depositors .. .. .. £103,921 at 4 per cent.
Due to Investing Shareholders .. £157,000 exclusive of Profits.
Due from Borrowing Shareholders .. £296,040 secured by Mortgages.

The Annual Balance Sheets show, by the increased funds entrusted to its care, that the public has had confidence in the Society's direction and management, and the results obtained fully justify such confidence.

The following are some of the advantages offered by this Society:—

### BORROWERS

May obtain at short notice advances upon security of land, houses, shops, works, &c., and facilities are given for redemption such as no private lender can possibly allow. Repayments may be made monthly, quarterly, or half-yearly, extending over from 5 to 14 years, to suit the Borrower's convenience, according to the following scale for each £100 advanced:—

| Term. | Monthly Repayment. | | | Annual Repayment. | | | Average Payments for Principal. | | | Interest. | | |
|---|---|---|---|---|---|---|---|---|---|---|---|---|
| 5 years | £1 | 19 | 1 | £23 | 9 | 0 | £20 | 0 | 0 | £3 | 9 | 0 |
| 7 " | 1 | 9 | 4 | 17 | 12 | 0 | 14 | 5 | 9 | 3 | 6 | 3 |
| 10 " | 1 | 2 | 2 | 13 | 6 | 0 | 10 | 0 | 0 | 3 | 6 | 0 |
| 12 " | 0 | 19 | 4 | 11 | 12 | 0 | 8 | 6 | 8 | 3 | 5 | 4 |
| 14 " | 0 | 17 | 6 | 10 | 10 | 0 | 7 | 2 | 10 | 3 | 7 | 2 |

At the expiration of the time selected by the Borrower, his payments cease absolutely; he may however, at any time at the discretion of the Directors, shorten or lengthen the term originally agreed upon, so as to increase or decrease his monthly payments.

Mortgages can be redeemed, wholly or in part, by payment of the present value of the repayments unpaid, discount being allowed at the rate of 5 per cent. per annum.

The usual commission is 5 per cent., and the Borrowers are not liable for any losses. The legal and Surveyor's charges are fixed by a low scale.

### INVESTORS.

There are two classes of Investing Shares, viz.:—

PAID-UP SHARES, which entitle the owner to £100 at the end of the selected term, with profits which have hitherto been equal to £18 for each 10 years' share. The charge for these shares varies from £68 for a 10 years' share to £83 for a 5 years' share. If withdrawn before maturity, 4 per cent. interest is allowed.

SUBSCRIPTION SHARES are similar to the above, whether they are paid by monthly or other periodical instalments ...

---

SURGICAL ELASTIC STOCKINGS, &c.

ESTABLISHED OVER HALF-A-CENTURY.

## W. A. SCOTT,
*(Successor to W. G. SNOWDON,)*

### Surgical Instrument,

ARTIFICIAL LIMB,

LADIES' BELT.

TRUSS & BANDAGE MANUFACTURER,

97a, NORFOLK-ST., and 2, HOWARD-ST.,

SHEFFIELD,

*Surgical Mechanician to the Sheffield Infirmary and Hospital, Rotherham Hospital, Chest... ... ... Public Institutions.*

---

Girls' Public Day School Company Limited,

IN CONNECTION WITH THE
NATIONAL UNION FOR IMPROVING THE EDUCATION OF WOMEN.

President of the Union:
HER ROYAL HIGHNESS PRINCESS LOUISE, MARCHIONESS OF LORNE.

President: THE EARL OF AIRLIE.

Chairman of the Council: W. H. STONE, Esq.

## SHEFFIELD HIGH SCHOOL,

SURREY STREET, SHEFFIELD.

HEAD MISTRESS - MRS. WOODHOUSE.

### THE AIM OF THE COMPANY

Is, by the employment of an ample staff of competent Teachers and the use of the best methods of instruction, to ensure for Girls an education adapted to their requirements, but as sound and thorough as that which Boys now receive in Grammar Schools of the highest class.

### THE SCHOOL COURSE

Includes Religious Instruction, Reading, Writing, Arithmetic and Mathematics, Bookkeeping, English Grammar, Composition and Literature, History, Geography, French, German, Latin, the Elements of Physical Science, Social Economy, Drawing, Class Singing and Harmony, Gymnastic Exercises and Needlework, or such of the above or other Subjects as the Council, with due regard to particular circumstances, may determine.

### THE SCHOOL YEAR

Is divided into Three Terms, each of about Thirteen Weeks.

### THE HOURS OF ATTENDANCE

Are from 9.30 to 1.30 every ... ... Saturday (which is a whole holiday). Regular and punctual atten... ... quired.
Lessons in Music, ... ... ... ... ... ... ons are given in the Afternoon.
The Pupils can ... ... ... ... ... be assisted by the Teachers to prepare their lessons ...

Top are shown old adverts for businesses once on Norfolk Street, and an old school once on Surrey Street

The decorative Sheffield and Hallamshire Savings Bank building on Norfolk Street was opened in 1860. It is now a bar but still has the lovely exterior intact, with the carvings shown above gracing the arches.

## The Victoria Hall

The Methodist preacher John Wesley held a service in Paradise Square in 1742. (A plaque marks a later service here in 1779, when he was heard to remark he had "never seen so many people on a weekday.")

**The tower of the Victoria Hall against a blue summer sky**

He called Sheffield people a 'shepherd without a sheep' and met a local preacher, David Taylor.

This meeting initiated the first Methodist Society in Sheffield. It was in a tiny meeting house in an area called Cheney Square.

Charles Wesley, John's brother, also came to Sheffield, a year later, and held a service with David Taylor in this tiny meeting house. A mob of people took against these meetings and the pair were stoned, with the wooden door of the meeting house being torn down. The riot act was read and the preachers went elsewhere to finish the meeting.

There were more riots against them in 1746, and the magistrates, having failed to keep peace, were ordered to meet the cost of building Methodists a chapel. This was built at Mulberry Street, where meetings were held peacefully, until 1779. By then a new, bigger place was needed. A new church on Norfolk Street was built in 1780, with John Wesley, then aged 77, leading the consecration service. By 1901, this was thriving and the Albert Hall, which stood in Barkers Pool, had to be hired sometimes to fit everyone in.

A new leader, the Rev George McNeal, arrived in 1905. He sometimes held open services in Fitzalan Square.

Eventually it was decided to build a bigger place to worship, on the site of the older Norfolk Street Chapel. A stone from this was used as a foundation stone for the new building, which was started in 1907. The new place was finished by 1913, complete with tower and a plaque showing the heads of the Wesley brothers on the front.

As well as for worship, this new building, named the Victoria Hall, was a major concert venue before the City Hall was built. Sometimes films were shown there too, and a Sunday School helped many children from the slums.

During the Second World War it was used as a Forces Rest Hostel, with camp beds set up inside.

Passing years brought many changes and by the 1960's it was decided to redesign the premises. Alterations and refurbishment took place in 1966.

**Left: Heads of the Wesley brothers on top of the hall frontage**

The Victoria Hall remains the city centre presence of the Methodist Church, with Sunday Services at 10.45am and 6.30pm and Thursday lunchtime worship. Doors are open seven days a week and the church is in constant use for numerous organisations and societies, with coffee served daily and a drop in centre.

**Telephone (0114) 2721749**

**Mother and child, George Fullard (1956)**

## Upper Chapel

Built in 1770, this Unitarian chapel is on Norfolk Street. The peaceful spot also provide a haven for many dinnertime sandwich breaks. Inside the chapel is a roomy but cosy space for worship.

In the grounds are sculptures by local artist George Fullard (1924-1973) sited here in 1985

They were originally plaster, bought by Sheffield City Council Arts Department in 1983 and cast into bronze in 1985.

# Around the City Hall

Sheffield City Hall was designed by architect Mr E Vincent Harris and opened September 1932.

## A grand venue

A long sweep of steps leads up to the impressive frontage of this well known city centre landmark set in Barkers Pool.

Building the City Hall, which opened in 1932, providing much needed work during the depression years.

It is built in the classical revival style, and its Corinthian colonnaded front and intricate iron gates have provided a grand welcome for the ballroom dancers, audiences and revellers that have visited here.

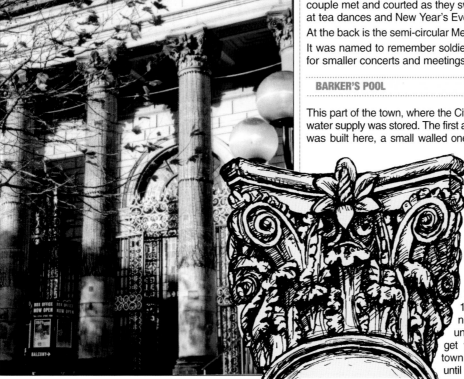

Inside, there are inside some lovely stained glass panels and a beautifully painted domed ceiling.

The main Oval Hall seats 2,300. The ceiling has a huge oval glass panel and carved stone roses and a round suspended light fitting that has loomed over thousands of heads. There are two horseshoe shaped balconies. curving around the walls.

Two Assyrian style stone lions used to sit either side of the Oval Hall stage, but conductors didn't like them, saying they spoiled acoustics and they were removed and sold to the Tarmac company in Matlock. for £600 the pair. Here they sat, until they were moved to the Tarmac head office in Wolverhampton in 1997. It is hoped they will eventually head back to Sheffield to once again take 'pride' of place here.

Below the Oval Hall is a grand ballroom where many a Sheffield couple met and courted as they swayed along to the orchestra at tea dances and New Year's Eve soirées galore.

At the back is the semi-circular Memorial Hall, which seats 550.

It was named to remember soldiers lost in battle. This is used for smaller concerts and meetings.

### BARKER'S POOL

This part of the town, where the City Hall stands, was where the water supply was stored. The first artificial reservoir for the public was built here, a small walled one. People fetched their water with pails. A gully ran from here down the middle of Fargate through into High Street and could be used to let water down to clean the streets, or to provide water if there was a fire.

This pool was named after a Mr Barker, who had made a large water storage holder here in the 15th century.

This pool was filled in about 1793, as it was said to be a nuisance but was probably unsanitary anyway. A pump to get water was built in 1825 by town trustees and was there until 1876.

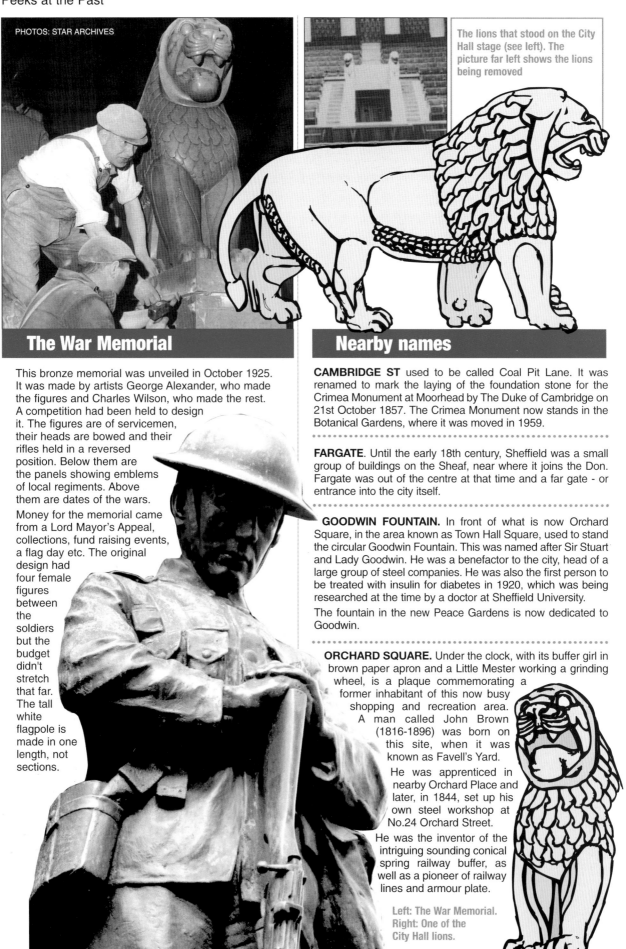

PHOTOS: STAR ARCHIVES

The lions that stood on the City Hall stage (see left). The picture far left shows the lions being removed

## The War Memorial

This bronze memorial was unveiled in October 1925. It was made by artists George Alexander, who made the figures and Charles Wilson, who made the rest. A competition had been held to design it. The figures are of servicemen, their heads are bowed and their rifles held in a reversed position. Below them are the panels showing emblems of local regiments. Above them are dates of the wars.

Money for the memorial came from a Lord Mayor's Appeal, collections, fund raising events, a flag day etc. The original design had four female figures between the soldiers but the budget didn't stretch that far. The tall white flagpole is made in one length, not sections.

## Nearby names

**CAMBRIDGE ST** used to be called Coal Pit Lane. It was renamed to mark the laying of the foundation stone for the Crimea Monument at Moorhead by The Duke of Cambridge on 21st October 1857. The Crimea Monument now stands in the Botanical Gardens, where it was moved in 1959.

**FARGATE**. Until the early 18th century, Sheffield was a small group of buildings on the Sheaf, near where it joins the Don. Fargate was out of the centre at that time and a far gate - or entrance into the city itself.

**GOODWIN FOUNTAIN.** In front of what is now Orchard Square, in the area known as Town Hall Square, used to stand the circular Goodwin Fountain. This was named after Sir Stuart and Lady Goodwin. He was a benefactor to the city, head of a large group of steel companies. He was also the first person to be treated with insulin for diabetes in 1920, which was being researched at the time by a doctor at Sheffield University.

The fountain in the new Peace Gardens is now dedicated to Goodwin.

**ORCHARD SQUARE.** Under the clock, with its buffer girl in brown paper apron and a Little Mester working a grinding wheel, is a plaque commemorating a former inhabitant of this now busy shopping and recreation area. A man called John Brown (1816-1896) was born on this site, when it was known as Favell's Yard.

He was apprenticed in nearby Orchard Place and later, in 1844, set up his own steel workshop at No.24 Orchard Street.

He was the inventor of the intriguing sounding conical spring railway buffer, as well as a pioneer of railway lines and armour plate.

Left: The War Memorial. Right: One of the City Hall lions.

## Leopold Street

### MEDICAL SCHOOLS

On Surrey Street and Arundel Street, there was an old medical school where the Central Library now stands. It opened in 1829 and had the latin motto 'Ars Longa, Vita Brevis' carved over the door. This is a quote from Hippocrates (400BC) which translates as, 'Art is Long, Life is Short.' You never stop learning, or having things to learn, no matter how long you live.

This sign is now by the bus terminal outside the Royal Hallamshire hospital. The school was at Surrey Street until 1888, than it moved to Leopold Street, to a school of Anatomy that had been started by a Dr Overend. The latin motto above is still over one of the old doorways to this school on Leopold Street today, at the Church Street end.

This old stone carved sign is found at the Fargate end of Leopold Street, high above what is now a jewellery shop.

It tells that the building used to be a cabinet makers. Later it used to be known as Beethoven House, the home of Wilson Peck music shop.

Above: Sign from the old school

At this time it was difficult to get corpses for medical research and so some people took to stealing them from graveyards and selling them. Rumours at the time said that Dr Overend was involved in this body snatching. All parts of the country had this problem. Famous body snatchers Burke and Hare operated in Edinburgh. Graveyards sometimes had watchtowers to look out for these corpse thieves, such as the one at Bradfield Church.

### CENTRAL SCHOOLS AND OFFICES

These were built in 1880 and were opened by Earl Spencer on 15th July. At the offices, the ground floor had a grand board room, with a decorated plaster ceiling and panels of carved oak. There were also store rooms, strong rooms, offices and a covered playground supported by stone columns for the children to use in wet weather. The Central Schools had a school of chemistry, a joiners' shop and an elaborate heating system in the basement. On the ground floor was a school of cookery, a junior school an infants' school, a gymnasium, and more classrooms.

The first floor held eight classrooms, head master and mistress rooms and a library. The second floor had a large hall which could accommodate 1,500 people. At the time there were many Little Mesters workshops still around the school, which would have made noise and probably proved a major distraction to learning. These were later demolished to make way for the Grand Hotel.

In March 1892, extensions were begun to the Central Schools and a new elementary school was erected in Holly Street. Additions included lecture rooms, chemical laboratories, a joiners' shop, a metalwork shop and a laundry. The new elementary school officially opened on April 22 1894.

In September 1910 the Central Secondary Schools became two separate schools, one for boys and one for girls.

### PUPIL TEACHERS' CENTRE

The Holly Building, on Holly Street at the back of the City Hall, opposite the Memorial Hall, was where the teachers were trained. It was opened in 1899 by the Duke of Devonshire

Left: Motto over the old medical school door on Leopold Street.
Above: an old print showing the Central Schools and Offices

# Firth College

What is now the Leopold Street area was part of several early street improvements by the Town Council. In 1874 it was announced that the area of land around Leopold Street was to be purchased by the Sheffield School Board.

At the time it was covered with houses shops and workshops. Mark Firth, a local steelmaker and industrialist, wanted to build a college there.

It was decided that he would pay the cost of building a college on part of the site, which would be named Firth College. Architects T R Flockton of Sheffield and E R Robson of London prepared plans for this college, as well as for the School Board's Central School and Offices on their part of the site.

The layout of the streets was completed in 1879, coinciding with the visit of Prince Leopold, who was in the city to open the new Firth College. It was therefore decided to call the street with the college on it after him. The opening was on October 18th. The entire cost of the construction, around £20,000, was paid for by Mark Firth. There were offices and a kitchen, and various sized lecture halls.

A new storey was added to the building in 1892, to provide more space for teaching. Money was raised by public subscription.

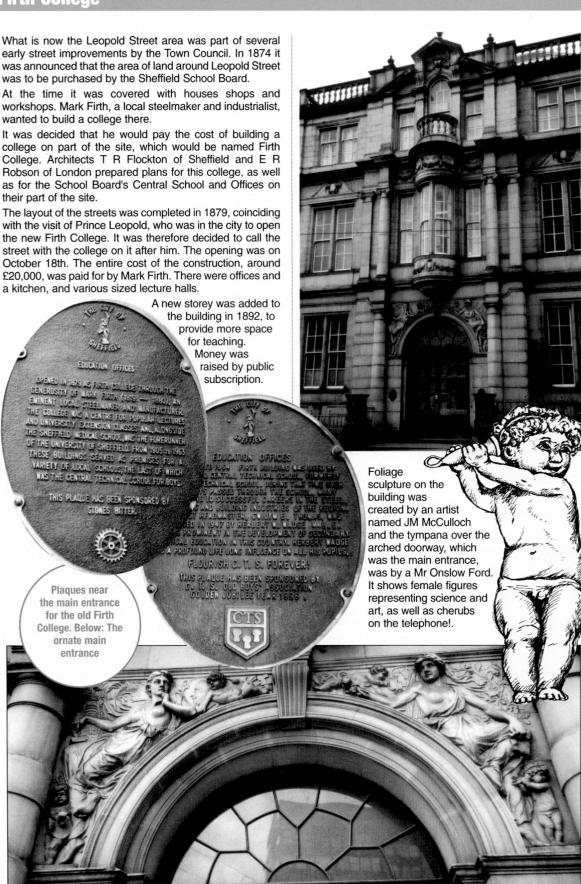

Plaques near the main entrance for the old Firth College. Below: The ornate main entrance

Foliage sculpture on the building was created by an artist named JM McCulloch and the tympana over the arched doorway, which was the main entrance, was by a Mr Onslow Ford. It shows female figures representing science and art, as well as cherubs on the telephone!.

# Ebenezer Elliott

**This poet, with his radical views and high ideals, used his work to protest against poverty, and high taxes on bread. He became known as The Corn Law Rhymer...**

Elliott was born at Masbrough, near Rotherham, in March 1781. His father was in the iron trade and at 16 he joined the family business.

*The Elliott monument at Weston Park*

### Nature lover

Though working in an industrial environment, Ebenezer was always looking to nature for recreation and inspiration. At just 17 he wrote his first poem, The Vernal Walk.

Ebenezer later took over the family business. He married, to a woman named Fanny Gartside, but life got difficult when the company hit hard times and he was left with no money and little future prospects there. He became bankrupt at the age of 36. To try and improve his luck, he decided to move the family to Sheffield. They were so poor the only transport they had was a cart, so they arrived in that. He borrowed money to start a new iron business in the city.

At the time, the so called Corn Laws were making it even harder for people to get enough to eat. There was an artificially high price for bread, a bread tax in all but name. Ebenezer was totally against this. He decided to protest, making his views known in political writings and poems. The most well known was 'The Corn Law Rhymes' which he wrote in 1831 and which earned him the name The Corn Law Rhymer. Also in 1831 an Anti-Corn Law League was formed and by 1846, the Corn Laws were repealed.

Many of Elliott's other poems reflect his love of the area around Sheffield. Among his most famous are The Village Patriarch, The Ranter and The Splendid Village. Many of his poems are set to music and the most well known is perhaps a hymn called The People's Anthem.

Ebenezer Elliott's other employment, the iron and steel business, began to do well at last and enabled him to move the family to a large house at Upperthorpe, at Blake Grove. This house is still there, at the end of Blakegrove Road.

"Elliott first wrote poetry as a poet, merely to please himself with the exercise of his talents; afterwards he made use of this godlike gift of Nature for a nobler purpose than even to obtain fame - he advocated the rights of the poor, whose labour is his life and denounced the oppressor, whose luxuries are wrongs."

Life of Ebenezer Elliott by John Watkins, his son in law

By the time he was 60, the firm was struggling again and Ebenezer decided to retire. He decided to leave the industrial heartland of Sheffield for the countryside and bought land at Great Houghton, Darfield, near Barnsley. Here he spent his last days, dedicating his last poem to a robin he saw beneath his window:

"Thy notes sweet robin soft as dew
heard soon or late are dear to me;
To music I could bid adieu, But not to thee.
When from my eyes this lifeful throng
has passed away, no more to be;
Then Autumn's primrose, robin's song
Return to me."

Ebenezer died in December 1849. He was buried in a quiet ceremony in Darfield churchyard.

## From THE RANTER

"Up! sluggards up! the mountains, one by one
Ascend in light and slow the mists retire
From vale and plain. The cloud on Stannington
Behold a rocket - No 'tis a Morthen spire.
The sun is risen cries Stanedge, tipped with fire.
On Norwood's flowers dew -drops shine and shake;
Up! sluggards up! and drink the morning breeze!
The birds on cloud-left Osgathorpe awake
And Wincobank is waving all his trees
Oe'r subject towns and farms and villages
And gleaming streams and woods and waterfalls.
"Up! climb the oak-crowned summit! Hoober Stand
And Keppel's Pillar gaze on Wentworth's halls

And misty lakes that brighten and expand,
And distant hills that watch the western strand.
Up! trace God's footprints where they paint the mould
With heavenly green and hues that blush and glow
Like angel's wings, while skies of blue and gold
Stoop to Miles Gordon on the mountain's brow.
Behold the Great Unpaid! the prophet. Lo!
Sublime he stands beneath the Gospel tree,
And Edmund stands on Shirecliffe at his side!
Behind him sinks and swells and spreads a sea
Of hills and vales and groves. Before him glide
Don, Rivelin, Loxley wandering in their pride
From heights that mix their azure with the cloud."

## Some more of Ebenezer Elliott's poems

### From THE PEOPLE'S ANTHEM

This is a well known hymn and will also be familiar to any fans of the musical Godspell...

"When will thy save the people?
Oh God of mercy! when?
Not kings and lords, but nations!
Not thrones and crowns, but men!
Flowers of thy heart, oh God, are they,
Let them not pass like weeds away!
Their heritage a sunless day!
God save the people!

Shall crime bring crime forever-
Strength aiding still the strong?
Is it thy will oh Father,
That men shall toil for wrong?
'No!' say thy mountains; 'No!" say thy skies;
'Man's clouded sun shall brightly rise
And songs be heard instead of sighs.
God save the people!"

### FAREWELL TO RIVELIN

Written when leaving Sheffield

"Beautiful River! Goldenly shining
Where, with the Cistus, Woodbines are twining.
Birklands around thee, Mountains above thee
Rivelin wildest! Do I not love thee!..."

He also wrote about climbing Win Hill:

"High on the topmost jewel of thy crown,
Win Hill! I sit bare-headed ancle deep
in tufts of rose - cupp'd bilberries; and look down
On towns that smoke below" ......

Elliott was also concerned that the family home should be a place of refinement and aesthetic appreciation, even if the people in it were too poor to buy the riches that others had. He wanted to encourage sensitivity and a love of beauty (and a lack of gin!) even in the harsh everyday world of the workers.

### THE HOME OF TASTE

"Oh, lift the workman's heart and mind
Above low sensual sin!
Give him a home! the home of taste!
outbid the house of gin!
Oh, give him taste! it is the link
Which binds us to the skies-
A bridge of rainbows thrown across
The gulph of tears and sighs;

This is also the theme in the poem SATURDAY:

"The fine folks use the plate he makes,
And praise it when they dine;
For John has taste - so we'll be neat,
Although we can't be fine."

It was decided to have a statue commemorating Elliott and £600 was collected by public subscription. The statue was made by an artist called Burnard and erected in Sheffield Market Place in August 1854. It was later moved, in 1875, to its present position in Weston Park (right), near Broomhill and the University. It shows Elliott holding corn in his hand, reference to his Corn Law Rhymes. He is seated on a rock, a favourite spot of his at Black Brook, near Manchester Rd.

### THE TAXED CAKE

"Give, give, they cry-
And take! for wilful men are they
Who tax'd our cake and
took our cake,
To throw our cake away.

The cake grows less and less,
For profits lessen too;
But land ill pay, at last, I guess,
For land-won Waterloo.
They mix our bread with bran,
They call potatoes bread;
And, get who may, or keep who can,
The starved, they say, are fed.

Our rivals fatten fast,
But we are free to pay;
And dearly they shall pay, at last,
Who threw our cake away".

### SONG

"Child, is thy father dead? Father is gone!
Why did they tax his bread? God's will be done!
Mother has sold her bed; better to die than wed!
Where shall she lay her head? Home we have none!

Father clamm'd thrice a week- God's will be done!
Long for work did he seek, Work he found none.
Tears on his hollow cheek Told what no tongue
could speak; Why did his master break?
God's will be done!

Doctor said air was best- Food we had none;
Father with panting breast, Groaned to be gone:
Now he is with the blest- Mother says death is best!
We have no place of rest- Yes, ye have one!"

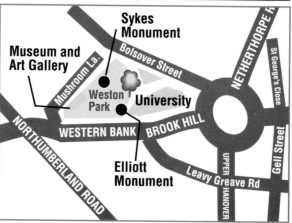

112

## Fletchers

A name famous in Sheffield and also associated with bread is that of the Fletcher family, the well known bakers. The life of a baker and their poor pay is a harsh reminder of the hardship that Elliot was writing about and trying to reform.

By May 1812, the price of bread and the bread tax, which Elliot was protesting against, was causing unrest. High prices for corn and flour meant that poor people were starving whilst the gentry selling the products made lots of profit. The laws repeal in 1846 meant life got a little better for the poor to buy bread for their families.

George Henry Fletcher was born in Horncastle in 1879. His father was a shoemaker, but was fond of drink and young George had to fend for himself a lot.

When he was a little older, he got himself a job at a windmill and bakers, but it was hard work and the bakers were often exhausted:

"men were bent over huge troughs, up to the armpits in dough..they caught dermatitis - for which they received no compensation. After mixing they were so tired that they often fell asleep on the trough lid, which when the dough had risen, pitched them on to the floor. Then they knew it was time to lift it out." *from Secret Ingredients book.*

Whilst working here at the mill he met and married a woman called Kate, from the slums of Brightside in Sheffield, where she worked as a maid. The hours worked at the mill were usually 6am to 6pm, with a break and then another short 45 minute stint later to get things ready for the next day. The pay was very low, about 20 shillings, (about £1 a week) compared to that of a file or razor cutter who got about 33 shillings. Sometimes the bakers were referred to as the 'white slaves of England.'

He decided to try and do better, moving to Derbyshire to try mining, but decided that was even harder. He and Kate decided to move to Sheffield, a boom town at the time, with trades expanding and people moving in and lots of work to be had. It was smoky and noisy, but they found a place in the North East side, in Danville Street. By this time they had four children, but the industrial grime took its toll and their first born boy died.

George Henry was working at a bakehouse called Simmerson, at nearby Clun Road, when Queen Victoria visited the city to open the new Town Hall. The bakers were supposed to have a treat of being taken around the streets to see the city's festive decorations as a reward for baking bread and cakes to feed the 50,000 school children that were assembled to meet the Queen in Norfolk Park. But the bakers were all so tired they fell asleep on route.

When refused a request for the shorter work of a 60 hour week George Henry decided it was best to leave and start his own bakery. It was a tiny place at 129 Gower Street, with hardly any facilities. With hard work and helpful neighbours they soon moved to a better place at Kirk Street.

His reputation for good bread (some bakers added chalk to the flour to bulk it out), meant the business did well, but conditions were still hard and unhealthy and a second of their children died. They decided to move back to Retford for the sake of the family's health, but a bakery there did not do well and they moved back to Sheffield. This time they got a place in a cleaner suburb, but after speaking out in public against hard conditions, George Henry ended up in jail and needed to go somewhere people knew him to survive, so they moved back to Gower Street.

Another child died in 1909, leaving one surviving son, George. Business improved and they moved to better premises at Staniforth Road in 1912.

During World War 1 the firm survived for the quality of its bread, refusing to bulk it out with potatoes as some other bakers did. By April 1923, the firm was known as Fletchers and Son and was at 82 Middlewood Road. They had also acquired a model T Ford car for deliveries. They did very well and doubled the size of their staff in two years.

The family bought land at Penistone Road to expand even further and were known to be good employers, having one of the first works canteens in the 1930s., as well as a contributory health scheme.
The last move was to premises at Claywheels Lane, a three acre site they bought in July 1945. George Henry died in 1958, but his son carried on the business. By 1959 they were making a quarter of a million loaves a week as well as confectionery, teacakes etc. They had 40 vans and 260 staff. George Junior died in 1973, but the firm, bigger still, carries on at the same Claywheels Lane site.

---

### CAGED RATS, another poem by Elliot against the Corn Laws

"Ye coop us up and tax our bread,
and wonder why we pine;
But ye are fat and round and red,
And filled with tax - bought wine:
Thus twelve rats starve while three rats thrive,
(Like you on mine and me)
When fifteen rats are caged alive,
With food for nine and three.

Haste! Havoc's torch begins to glow-
The ending is begun;
Make Haste! Destruction thinks ye slow;
Make haste to be undone!
Why are ye called'my Lord' and 'Squire'
While fed by mine and me
And wringing food and clothes and fire
From bread taxed misery?

# The City Museum and Art Gallery

Wealthy Industrialist John Newton Mappin begin the chain of events that gave birth to the Sheffield City Art gallery at Weston Park, by leaving money in his will. He was born in 1800 and later on in his life set up a brewery on Ecclesall Road, which eventually became the now closed Wards Brewery. He became wealthy enough to move to a large house in Ranmoor and also use money to build up his art collection.

His first gift to the city was a stained glass window in the then parish church, in 1865. This was given in memory of the poet and hymn writer James Montgomery. He died in 1883 and left wishes that the money be used to build somewhere to hold and display his now large art collection.

His wishes came to fruition and the new Mappin Art Gallery was opened on July 27, 1887. JN Mappins' nephew, Sir Frederick Thorpe Mappin presented the gallery, his uncle's collection and some of his own paintings to the city. Sir Henry Stephenson, the Mayor, accepted it.

The Mappin Art Gallery was built adjacent to the recently established City Museum, already on the site. This museum was a conversion of a house belonging to a Miss Harrison, whose estate was known as Weston Park. The house was purchased by the city in 1873, with the museum opening in 1875.

The new art gallery was praised by many and a great success, but by the 20's it had grown a little old fashioned. It was in 1929 that Mr Graves gave money for a new gallery and library in the centre of the town and so they also had more rivalry. In consequence the Mappin was revamped and extended, reopening in April

1937 with a new more modern look, new staircase etc.

In the World War II Sheffield Blitz in the December of 1940, the museum and art gallery suffered extensive damage. A parachuted landmine went through the glass roof and exploded. Much had to be demolished for safety. Works of art were moved elsewhere for safety.

It was agreed that the place should be rebuilt and after extensive work it was reopened in June 1965.

Now at time of writing in 2002, more grand plans for the museum and art gallery are underway, with a new layout, bigger cafe and more interactive exhibits.

**Telephone: 0114 278 2600**

**www.sheffieldgalleries.org.uk**

Frieze of Sheffield Industry from the Museum wall

## THE MUSEUM

The relief carvings on the main entrance to the City Museum were designed by the artist Tory and their firm of architectural stonemasons and completed in 1937. They had already done work for the City Library and Art Gallery in the city centre. The subject was described in the programme for the official opening of the new City museum and Art Gallery in April 1937. It is said to symbolise the purpose of the museum, showing the shrine of knowledge with four steps leading up to it. The steps are carved with animals indicating the order of their appearance in time-Crustaceans, Fishes, Reptiles and Mammals, with birds in flight around the altar. Figures at the sides bring gifts from overseas. Another frieze on the east side indicates men at work in Sheffield's heavy industries.

The impressive frontage of the Art Gallery

## SYKES MONUMENT

In the park is a fine tall column. This is a memorial to the artist Godfrey Sykes (1824-1866). He trained and then taught at Sheffield School of Art, later moving to London to work on the decorations on the Victoria and Albert Museum. The panels on the monument show the 'Three Ages of Man'. The gateposts (lower) in the Western bank side of the park are copies of ones in the V& A quadrangle, where Sykes was working when he died. There are also plaques, showing an artist's brushes and palette, a portrait of Sykes, and one bearing these words,"Godfrey Sykes born at Malton in the year 1824. A pupil and afterwards master in the school of art of this town". He was called to London in the year 1859 to superintend the decoration of the South Kensington Museum and died there in 1866".

# Bibliography and suggested reading

**Barrows in England and Wales.**
Leslie V. Grinsell  Shire Archaeology
ISBN 0 85263 669 5

**The Peak District - Landscapes Through Time**
John Barnatt & Ken Smith
ISBN 0 77134 7529 3

**Arbor Low - a guide to the monuments**
Peak National Park Publications
ISBN 0 9075 43 74 X

**The Burial Mounds of Derbyshire**
BM Marsden 1977

**Carved in Bright Stone**
Derbyshire Museum Service
ISBN 0 906 753120

**Prehistory in the Peak**
Mark Edmonds and Tim Seabourne
ISBN 0 75241483 6

**The Illustrated Guide To Sheffield. 1879** Pawson and Brailsford
(cost then 2/6)
An old guide to the city and surrounding area, complete with lovely old etchings and advertisements

**Vestiges of the Antiquities of Derbyshire,**
Thomas Bateman 1848

**Ten Years' Diggings in Celtic and Saxon Grave Hills in the Counties of Derby, Stafford and York**
Thomas Bateman 1861

**The Barrow Knight**
About Thomas Bateman
B. M. Marsden 1988

**Derbyshire Origins**
Sheffield City Museums

**Curiosities of the Peak District,**
Frank Rodgers
ISBN 0 903485 47 8

**Historic Hallamshire**
David Hey
ISBN 1 84306 049 3

**Sheffield in Tudor and Stuart Times**
Sheffield City Museums
ISBN 0863210317

**Sheffielders- A life in the City**
George Shaw

**Forging the Valley**
David Hey, Martin Olive and Martin Liddament
ISBN 1 - 85075-647-3

**Buffalo Bill's British Wild West**
Alan Gallop
ISBN 0 7509 27 02 X
History of William Cody's tour of Edwardian and Victorian Britain between 1887 and 1903

**A Popular History of Sheffield**
J E Vickers
ISBN 071581241-6

**History & Guide, Chesterfield**
Geoff Sadler
ISBN 0 7524 2451 3

**The Story of Paradise Square**
Alan Hall
ISBN 086 3211 259

**Lost Sheffield-Portrait of a Victorian City**
Peter Machan
ISBN 1 901 587 12 6

**The Making of the South Yorkshire Landscape**
Melvyn Jones   ISBN 1-871647 75 4

**The Sheffield Blitz**
Paul License   ISBN 095 39750 0 2

**The Definitive A-Z of Sheffield Public Houses**
Michael Liversidge
ISBN 09534267 - 1- 8

**Two Sheffield Poets**
(James Montgomery and Ebenezer Elliot)
Rev. Canon Odom 1829

**Memoirs of Ebenezer Elliot**
January Searle 1852 (2nd edition)

**Ebenezer Elliott, Corn Law Rhymer and Poet of the Poor**
Ray Hearne and Keith Morris
A new book for 2002

**Water Power on the Sheffield Rivers**
Edited by David Crossley
ISBN 0 950660 12 4

**Listed Buildings in Sheffield**
Barbara A West
ISBN 187471832 6

**Secret Ingredients, The Story of Fletchers' Seven Bakeries**
Howard Hill
ISBN 0 7158 12637

**History in the Baking Fletchers 75 Years 1923-1998**
(An updated version of the above book, revised and extended by Richard Woolley)

**Leaven of Life The Story of George Henry Fletcher**
Nellie Connole (1961)

**Sheffield's Citadel**
Paul Wileman
ISBN 18747 18342

**Old Sheffield Town**
J Edward Vickers
ISBN 085409 7740

**Edward Carpenter: Prophet of Human Fellowship,**
Chushichi Tsuzuki ISBN 0 521 2337 12
**Plus** numerous of Carpenter's own writings, kept in the Sheffield Archives, including My Days and Dreams, autobiographical notes.

**Socialism and the New Life:**
Sheila Rowbottom and Jeffrey Weeks
ISBN 0 904383 52 0

**All Their Yesterdays -**
(a history of Millthorpe):
Bessie Bunker

**The Worm in the Bud**
Ronald Pearsall (About Victorian Sexuality,
including Edward Carpenter)
ISBN 0140063439

**Remote and Undisturbed A Brief History of the Sheffield General Cemetery**
Jane Horton
ISBN 0 9539994 0 8

**She lived unknown, A celebration of women in the General Cemetery**
Julia Duggleby and Jean Lees
ISBN 0 953999424

**Goodbye The Wicker**
A R Fearney
ISBN 09539401.01

**A Laymans Look at the History and Industry, People and Places of Oughtibridge, Worrall and Wharncliffe**
Doug Sanderson

**Sheffield Walkabout**
Stephen McClarence and Norah Rodgers
ISBN 086321 0856

**The Lords House**
Catholic buildings in South Yorkshire
Denis Evinson
ISBN 185075 303 2

**Totley and the Tunnel**
Brian Edwards
ISBN 0952506416

**The Early Years of Cinema in Sheffield 1896-1911**
Clifford H Shawe and Stuart R Smith
ISBN 09526036-08

**Padley Chapel**
Barbara M Smith
ISBN 086384 2089

**The Dramatic Story of the Sheffield Flood**
Peter Machin

**Put Yourself in his Place**
Charles Reade
A splendid old Victorian novel of grinding, rattening, unions, love and a flood. Inspired by true historical events in Sheffield

**Ivanhoe**
Walter Scott
A historical novel which features the areas around Sheffield and Conisbrough Castle.

**A Wander Up the 'Cliffe**
Michael Liversidge
Memories of Attercliffe

**Notable Churches of Derbyshire**
Robert Innes Smith
ISBN 0 85 100 072

**Strange Sheffield**
Legends and spooky goings on in the area
David Clarke and Rob Wilson

**The Green Man**
Kathleen Basford
ISBN 0 859 91 497 6

**The Green Man**
William Anderson
ISBN 0 00 599 255 9

**The Little Book of the Green Man**
Mike Harding
ISBN 1 854 10 563 9

**The Anglo Saxon Chronicles**

**The A - Z of Dore**
John Dunstan and Roger Millican
ISBN 0 9534267 6 9

**A History of Birley Spa**
Leonard Widdowson
A booklet about the old spa baths

**Collins Gem Guide to Wild Flowers**
Marjorie Blamey and Ricard Fitter
ISBN 0 00 458 801 0

Ideal for sticking in the pocket when wandering around graveyards etc.

**At the Heart of the City**
Nicholas Farr
ISBN 0 95 173 320 6
The story of the Victoria Hall.

## Thanks to...

**Paul Barnatt-** Peak District Archaeology
**Robin Fielder** - Kelham Island Museum
**Nick Howe-** Sheffield Anglican Cathedral Chaplain
**Father Desmond,** St Maries Cathedral
**Paul Wilson,** Verger, Chesterfield Parish Church
**Rev. Jepps,** St Peter's, Conisbrough
**Rev. Canon Trevor Paige-,** Bradfield Church
**Trevor Pearson and Keith Mille**r, English Heritage
**Kim Streets**- Sheffield City Museum
**Herbert Challis**
**SWAT**
**John Pilkington,** Conisbrough Castle Visitor Centre
**Julie MacDonald** - Archivist, Cutlers Hall
**Edward Baker**
**Cath Parker**
**Nicola Hale**
**Peter Harvey**
**Anne Marie,** Fletcher's Bakery
**Paul Fletcher**
**The Star Newspaper**
**Stephen Gay**
**Keith Derbyshire** Dilys Guite Players
**Roy Higginbottom**

**Fred Meggitt**
**Gordon Gollogher**
**James Lant-** Hancock & Lant
**Local History Library staff**
**Jan Alton** - Medical Herbalist
**Rev George Barton** Victoria Hall
**Mr Archdale** Sharrow Snuff Mills
**Anne-Marie Knowles -** Chesterfield Museum and Art Gallery
**June Pettitt -** Fulwood Old Chapel
**Graham and Judy Hague**
**Sue Nelson**
**Barbara M. Smith** - Honourary Custodian, Padley Chapel
**Phil Skelton** - Landlord of Carbrook Hall
**Henk Littlewood** - Friends of the General Cemetery
**Ros Hancock** - Friends of the Porter Valley
**Eddie & Kath Greenwood**
**Mark Collins** Hall/Carpenter Archives
**Simon Dawson** The Edward Carpenter Archive
**Richard Foster -** Friends of Manor 'Castle'
**David Saville**
**Paul Wileman**
**Sally Pereira**

*and anyone I have spoken with or had help from whom I may have neglected to mention*

## Useful websites, addresses & telephone numbers

www.hendersons-relish.co.uk
www.snuffs-r-us.com
(Wilsons Snuff Mills)
www.carbrookhall.co.uk
www.sheffieldtoday.net
(The Star Newspaper's website)
www.simt.co.uk
(Sheffield Industrial Museums trust)
www.tilthammer.com
A site about local people and industry
www.sheffield-cathedral.org.uk
(Sheffield Anglican Cathedral)
www.stmariecathedral-sheffield.org
(Sheffield Catholic Cathedral)
www.conisbroughcastle.org.uk
www.english-heritage.org.uk
Tel: (0870) 333 1182
www.stonepages.com
(featuring ancient archaeology, stone circles etc including Arbor Low panoramic photographs)
www.genuki.org.uk
(Sheffield Places, photos etc.)
www.oldheeley.supanet.com
(Heeley history workshop)
www.upperchapel.freeserve.co.uk
Unitarian Chapel, Norfolk St. Sheffield)
www.sorby.org.uk
Sorby Natural History Society
www.picturesheffield.com
(A collection of old photographs from the library archives)
www.simondsn.dircon.co.uk
(Edward Carpenter Archive)

www.hallcarpenter.tripod.com
(Hall/Carpenter Archives)
www.shu.ac.uk
(Public Art Archive)
www.victorian-society.org.uk
Tel: (020) 8994 1019
■ **Friends of the General Cemetery,** (www.fogc.org)
The Lansdowne Chapel
104 Cemetery Road, Sheffield S11 8FP
(0114) 2798402
■ **Friends of Manor 'Castle'**
(0114) 2652151 or 2690615
■ **South Yorkshire Industrial History Society**
(0114) 2361471
■ **Fletchers Bakery**
Claywheels Lane (0114) 2348171
■ **Markets Customer Information**:
(0114) 2736245
■ **Sheffield Archives**
52 Shoreham Street
Sheffield S1 4SP (0114) 2039395
■ **Hendersons Relish**: 0114 2725909
■ **Hancock and Lant,**
Lady's Bridge, Sheffield S3 8GB
(0114) 272 2176
■ **Public Art Slide Library**,
David Ball 2252721
■ **Friends of the Porter Valley**:
(0114) 2302247
■ **Sheffield Visitor Information Centre**:
(0114) 2211900
■ **Sheffield Central Lending Library**
(0114) 2734729

■ **Sheffield Museum and Art Gallery:**
(0114) 2782600
■ **Chesterfield, Our Lady and All Saints (Crooked Spire): (**01246) 206506
■ **Chesterfield Tourist Information:** (01246) 345777
■ **Chesterfield Borough Museum,** St Mary's Gate: (01246) 345727
■ **Alton & James Medical Herbalists** 253 Sharrowvale Road, S11 8ZE
Telephone (0114) 2682468
■ **Cutlers' Hall, Sheffield**
(0114) 2728456
■ **Lantern Theatre**
(0114) 2551776
■ **Sheffield Theatres**
(Lyceum and Crucible)  (0114) 2495999

*What life is this, if, full of care, we have no time to stop and stare*

*Stone faces peer from corners; a winged dragon perches lightly on a sill.*

*Forgotten hands that wrought them give us pleasure still*